WHEN A LOVED ONE DIES

How to go on without saying goodbye

HANS STOLP

Translated by Jaap Hiddinga

BOOKS

Winchester, UK
New York, USA

WHEN A LOVED ONE DIES

Copyright © 2005 O Books
O Books is an imprint of John Hunt Publishing Ltd., The Bothy,
Deershot Lodge, Park Lane, Ropley, Hants, SO24 0BE, UK
office@johnhunt-publishing.com
www.o-books.net

Distribution in:

UK
Orca Book Services
orders@orcabookservices.co.uk
Tel: 01202 665432   Fax: 01202 666219 Int. code (44)

USA and Canada
NBN
custserv@nbnbooks.com
Tel: 1 800 462 6420   Fax: 1 800 338 4550

Australia
Brumby Books
sales@brumbybooks.com
Tel: 61 3 9761 5535   Fax: 61 3 9761 7095

New Zealand
Peaceful Living
books@peaceful-living.co.nz
Tel: 64 7 57 18105   Fax: 64 7 57 18513

Singapore
STP
davidbuckland@tlp.com.sg
Tel: 65 6276   Fax: 65 6276 7119

South Africa
Alternative Books
altbook@global.co.za
Tel: 27 011 792 7730   Fax: 27 011 972 7787

Text: © 2003 Hans Stolp
Originally published under the title *Als een geliefde sterft* by Ankh-Hermes
© Ankh-Hermes bv, Deventer, the Netherlands

Design: Graham Whiteman Design
Cover design: Krave Ltd., London

ISBN 978 1 903816 95 0

A CIP catalogue record for this book is available from the British Library.

Printed and bound by CPI Group (UK) Ltd, Croydon, CR0 4YY

ABOUT THE AUTHOR

Hans Stolp is a pastor and author. He is connected to the society "de Heraut" and gives lectures and courses on esoteric Bible readings, angels, the mystery tradition, dealings with deceased, and many other subjects which are connected with New Age thinking.

He is also editor of the quarterly magazine *Verwachting* (expectation). You ccan find more information on the website of the society "de Heraut": www.heraut.myweb.nl or on his own website: www.hansstolp.nl.

CONTENTS

For Dicky

Loss came
As a thunder strike
From one moment
To the next
It became completely dark

You had no choice
You went searching and feeling
Right through the gorges
Of despair
And desperation

You lost and won
Because on that journey
Insight was born
A deeper knowledge
The true source of life
Was unlocked

Now you live
From this wealth
Which was born
In the dark

Loss and gain
But the greatest gain
Is to know
That love is everlasting

Because love
Never dies

*I*NTRODUCTION

orrow – none of us will be spared. Sooner or later it will enter our lives.

Often it is connected with the loss of a loved one – either through death or through separation. When we are left behind the distress that we experience can be the most extreme sorrow in our lives on earth. We are so close to our loved ones, so intense from heart to heart in all our deepest senses, that a parting from the beloved person will touch us in our innermost being and can tear us apart. We die a little in ourselves when a loved one dies. You could say that in our heart we die a little when we bid farewell to our beloved. Our heart is the most vulnerable part of our whole being and our personality, and so sorrow is experienced there at its sharpest. In particular, our heart knows itself torn apart, when we have to say goodbye to a loved one to whom all our love goes out.

orrow – none of us will be spared. Sooner or later it will enter our lives.

There are many forms of sorrow: apart from the loss of a loved one, it is also possible to experience sorrow over the loss of a job, which you liked and which provided security, or sorrow when you lose your health and become incapacitated. You feel sadness when your dog dies. Sorrow originates always in a loss: of a loved one, your good health, your job, or an animal. There are many kinds of sorrow according to the poet Vasalis, but the factor common to all of them, she maintains, is that the actual process of cutting of the bond of love is not the most painful element, but the fact that one is cut off from the object of love.

As times passes, the pain of the loss, the sadness, and the loneliness is experienced in an intense manner within the essence of your heart. Indeed it increases, and becomes even more painful, than the original shock when the loss was first experienced.

Sorrow – none of us will be spared. Sooner or later it will enter our lives.

But whatever loss caused this sorrow, we have to deal with it, whether we like it or not. In order to survive it is essential that we do so. We have to experience and live through the process and, step by step, digest it. That is why each loss begins with the hard work of what is often called the grieving process. Freud used this term for the first time in 1912, when he called it "trauerarbeit." He meant, with this expression, that we have to work hard to heal the sorrow, and grow above this feeling and pain. "Grieving process" sounds like a technical term, but hidden away beneath the surface of these words is a world of emotions, sadness, and loneliness.

This book deals with the way we go step by step though the process of sorrow and sadness; how do most people deal with it? What will they experience in such a period? What phases will they live through? Of course, every human being is unique and every person will deal with sorrow in their own unique and personal way. Yet there is a common thread detectable in how we humans handle the grieving process. Insight into this thread can therefore provide insight into the process one has to go through when sorrow enters a person's life. It can provide encouragement, a firmer grip, and even consolation or comfort. You discover that it is not as strange as you might think to experience this chaos of emotions. You discover that you are not mad, but the chaos of emotions, which appear to make you mad, are part of the process you are going through. You discover that there is the prospect of emerging from the sorrow as a stronger and different person. You discover that you have many brothers and sisters who have lived through the same process. That is why insight into the grieving process, which you experience as a human being when you are forced to say goodbye to a loved one, can provide encouragement and consolation.

No one can take away the sorrow of someone else. We cannot protect each other from sadness and sorrow. But we can help each other to deal with it. We can encourage and hold each other. One of these encouragements is that we can provide each other with insight into what actually happens to a person living through the deep pain of sorrow. This book is aimed at providing people who go through the grieving process with these essential insights and encouragements.

But it is also meant for people who want to feel and understand what the other person experiences in this process of sorrow – because we all meet people who have lost a loved one not so long ago. How do you react? What can you say, or rather, what should you not say? What can we possibly do for the other person? Insight into the grieving process can help us to understand the other person and, where possible, to provide support. That is essential, since, although the taboo on talking about death may be broken, the taboo on sorrow is still with us in a big way. An example of such a taboo is the following: often it is assumed that two years after the loss of the loved one a person is finally over it. We assume that they are open to life and that they have learned in those two years to let go of the past. Many react in this way to someone who has lost a loved one, say two years ago. "Are you over it now?" they will ask in a friendly way.

But everyone who has lost a loved one knows that often after two years the feelings of being lost, lonely, and sorrowful are sometimes more ingrained and sharper than ever before. It is almost as if our soul requires those two years to realize that it is really true, the other person will never come back. It is as if we require two years to feel the depth of our despair, to actually let those emotions really go in ourselves.

Two years after the loss of the loved one (generally speaking, since the length of the process differs from person to person) the pain and the sorrow is at its peak. While others will tell you "You are over it now," you will feel incredibly lonely since such a remark will make clear that the other person does not really understand what is going on inside you. Insight into the grieving process can therefore help bystanders to react more sensitively, and with understanding, and through this they can be a support for the grieving person.

Our time is clearly a time of doing everything quickly. This tendency has no place in the process of grieving. A grieving process requires time, lots of time, and this process requires its own dynamics, its own pace: a pace which cannot be accelerated even though you may want to speed things up. It means that people who are going through a grieving process cannot function properly for a while. They are not really "with it" and are, in economic terms, not very efficient workers for a while. In our time-is-money society this is almost a mortal sin. Respect for the big life task of dealing with the deep sorrow resulting from a loss, can ensure that we as a community can provide the space and time to someone who has to deal with this. What becomes important is the person in need, rather than the economic value someone may have for the community.

Someone who has a visible sorrow about a loved one who has died is, to an extent, also a threat to their surroundings. Through that very obvious feeling of sorrow the other person will remind us of death and also of the irreversible way death can enter our lives. Besides, we do not really know what to say to someone who harbors a deep sadness. That is the reason why we often try to avoid such a person. Often, people who have lost a loved one report that acquaintances they meet in the supermarket will at first pretend that they do not see them. They dive away in the alley, or start to look with feigned interest at a product, just to avoid the meeting. We are so afraid of death, that we feel helpless when we are close to someone who experiences intense sorrow. Insight into the grieving process can contribute to conquering those fears and, through this process, we can be a real support and help for the other person. We should learn to see the other person no longer as a threat but as someone who can teach us something: how one can go through the dark path of our lives and re-merge as a new being.

Fear will then be replaced by respect. We don't need to say anything to people in sorrow. We only need to open our heart and listen.

The inner guide

For years I have worked as a pastor to guide people who have lost a loved one through death. In this work something special occurred to me that has touched me deeply. In the beginning I felt that as a counselor I should give advice and provide all sorts of things that made sense, to help the other person to deal with the grief. But I soon discovered that the other person was not really waiting for advice, but rather for my silence. When I looked deeper into this, I learned to see that such people carry a deep inner force, which functioned rather like an inner guide. Often they were not conscious of the fact that this was within them. And yet their own impulses, their own spontaneous inspiration, their dreams, and their own words showed that this inner guide was indeed within them. I realized more and more that, as a pastor, I only needed to come across this guide, lead people to awareness of it, and help them to follow their inner voice. This inner guide is the best guide one can think of to guide people step by step through their own grieving process in their own very personal way.

This has taught me how much we are guided and that the only issue is that we are aware of this guide and follow it in its directions. I know that what I am about to say cannot be proved. The work of the guide is too subtle and too deep within us. We can't point a finger to it and say, "That is it." But for those who with love, compassion, and care can listen to people who have experienced the sorrow, the guide will become obvious and clear. Those people will be impressed by the help available from the spiritual world, help that often comes from unexpected quarters. I learned very quickly that I could trust this force, since it is this force that guides everyone through the dark, step by step. It helps them to become aware of their pain and their sorrow, to deal with it and to let go. It is this force that provides insight to those who are left behind, that love cannot die, and we are always connected through love, even though we are separated through the physical death. It meant for me that I could be with people in their deepest despair without the need to do something, but just to be there for them. The help did not come from me, but from the inner spiritual force that is in every individual, even though we are not always aware of it.

A deciding life crisis

The manner in which we deal with our sorrow will determine the rest of our lives. If we do not deal with it correctly, then it can make us cynical, bitter, and hard. This cynicism originates from a variety of emotions of anger (to God, to life, or even to the loved one who left us behind by dying), which we did not allow ourselves to feel, preferring to suppress it in a hidden corner in our soul. It is very difficult to allow this irrational feeling of anger to be projected on to the loved one who died. The person who died cannot help it. They did not do this on purpose. In short, our logical thinking will replace that irrational emotion of anger lurking in the hidden corner. But it does not lie dormant; whatever was hidden away will work through our soul. It will re-emerge in a different way and often in the form of cynicism to the people around us. We will react with that cynicism to what is in the newspaper or on television. It is the hidden exhaust pipe of emotions of anger, which we won't let in consciously, or even willingly acknowledge.

We become bitter, as we remain stuck in the question of "why?" Why did the other person have to (so young or so early) die? This bitterness will arise when we cannot grow through the depth of our sorrow toward a form of answer, a form of insight, and if we do not grow through the dark toward a "that's why." That answer can only emerge through the deepest darkness of our despair: in the deepest dark light will be born. But if we do not allow ourselves those feelings of despair, because they are heavy or too severe, and if we suppress our emotion by immersing ourselves in our work, for example, then they can transform into a bitterness within our souls.

Ten years after the death of her husband I had a conversation with a woman. During this conversation she said: "I do not understand why my husband had to die so young. I do not think it fair. If I go somewhere I always see people who are together whilst I am always alone. I don't think it is fair that I had to lose my husband so young whilst others are allowed to be together for so long." This woman lived through the pain, and pushed her sorrow away, but she had not dealt with it, and therefore it had become bitterness.

If we remain stuck in the grieving process, then not only can a form of cynicism come into our lives, but also a certain hardness or an emotionless condition. Those people who do not allow themselves to feel through the emotions of despair, sorrow, and loneliness cannot feel again the emotions of happiness and gratitude. Those who cannot feel joy or sorrow will become hard and lacking in emotion.

But there is another way – and thankfully this happens often. It is possible that we emerge from our life crisis as whole new beings. The person who discovers that they can live through the deepest loneliness without permanent damage will emerge with new-found confidence. Those who have found in their darkest hour the inner answer to the question of the meaning of life and death, will emerge from the life crisis as a whole new person, a person with answers and insights, which are real answers and insight, and no one can ever take this away.

Often people discover something very special in that deepest darkness, namely that they feel carried by a wondrous force even though their own spiritual strength has been lost.

I cannot put it in any other words than this: many people will experience in their sorrow great spiritual forces which will help them and support them in many different ways. Everyone who has experienced this will wake up as a new being from this life crisis. They know that we, as human beings, are never alone but that, should we fall, we will always be picked up – although this may not happen in the time we want, but in a time that is deemed to be the correct time from a spiritual point of view. That insight, this inner wealth, is the greatest profit a human being can gain from the darkness of life, and will make us forever human beings with a new-found confidence, a new respect, and a new-found gratitude.

The way we go through the grieving process is therefore a determining factor for the rest of our future on earth, and for the human being who will emerge from this life crisis. That is one of the reasons for paying so much attention to the grieving process.

This book will emphasize the way we can deal with the loss of a loved one. But everyone who deals with a loss of some sort can recognize the description, since the grieving process that we experience with any loss will always follow similar patterns. I hope that this book will be a comfort to all readers who experience a loss, and will provide insight to all who have to deal with someone who has experienced loss.

SO PALE AND SILENT

So pale and silent you lie there
I cannot yet comprehend
I still hear your voice
I see the silent smile
In which you looked at me in silence

So pale and silent you lie there
I cannot yet comprehend
I do see, but I think
That suddenly you will
Open your eyes
And look at me with a smile
As if this was just a joke

So pale and silent you lie there
I cannot yet comprehend
Where have you gone?
Is there a new scene
Which opened for your eyes?
There, beyond the last frontier?

So pale and silent you lie there
I cannot yet comprehend

I.

*T*HE SHOCK

The most difficult life task

When a loved one dies, the ground falls away from under our feet. We are shocked and bewildered to the deepest depth of our being. We cannot comprehend it, and have the feeling that we ourselves die a little with our loved one. The loved person can be our husband or wife, or our partner. It is also possible that it can be one of our children, one of our parents, or a friend who was very dear to us, or even a well-loved pet. But whatever our relationship is with the loved one, whenever someone dies with whom we have an emotional bond, our world will collapse.

Dreams can show us meaningful images during the process of death of the loved individual. Dreams of an earthquake, a solar eclipse, or an avalanche – and these images will express very clearly what is happening with the person who is left behind. The solar eclipse will take the light of our life away and will bring darkness, and in this darkness there will be in turn a chill and a feeling of loneliness. The sun, which gave us warmth, light, and happiness, has set. It is now dark, and we cannot see anything at all. We cannot find the way in the dark, and cannot see others around us. We feel completely lost, alone, helpless, and desperate.

The image of the earthquake is a clear image of what will happen to us when a loved one dies: the ground will shake under our feet, the old world we knew and trusted has collapsed, and we do not know how to run for safety. And then there is the dream image of the avalanche. We find ourselves in a beautiful mountain landscape, in virginal snow and breathtaking beauty, which will touch us in the deepest recesses of our heart. But then, very suddenly, in the blink of an eye, this beauty will change into a terrifying nightmare. An avalanche will erupt and destroy everything in its path. The once so beautiful and touching world is now a world full of threats, destruction, and danger. The superior forces of nature make us feel tiny and helpless.

Whether our loved one dies unexpectedly or whether we are prepared for this, in both cases the shock is overwhelming. Often outsiders see the approach of someone's death long before it happens, but those who are closest still write in their bereavement announcements that the death was "sudden and unexpected." Even if we have been preparing ourselves before our loved one died, we are often faced with the fact that we have not really been able to prepare ourselves and that we could not imagine the emotions which would overwhelm us when the end of the earth life of our loved one has finally come. We knew in our mind that everything would change and that there would be a time when we would be alone, without the warmth and love of our dearest. But now it appears that we did not know this with our heart. We were unable to contemplate the emotions, which the death of our dearest would actually bring us. Moreover, as long as our loved one was still alive, we also gave love, attention, and care. We had to be strong for the other person and now, when it is not required anymore, all those emotions which we hid away, since we had to be strong, suddenly surface. And when those feelings of despair, sadness, powerless, and loneliness also surface then it appears to be that those emotions are much stronger and have much more impact then we could ever have contemplated in our mind.

Everyone who has experienced this knows – and the dream images confirm this – that to deal with the death of a loved person is one of the hardest experiences life on this earth can throw at us. Looking back people say that life was different before the death of the loved one. The death of the loved one is therefore a life-changing and determining event. Moreover, to have to deal with the loss is a life task, which we did not ask for. Whether you want it or not, it will just happen to you. But when it happens to you, you have no choice other than to go through with it, right through the despair, fear, sadness, and whatever other emotions will overwhelm us in such a position. You cannot avoid it. You have to deal with it in your own way.

In our present society we must also look at the fact that we do not always lose our partners to death, but also through divorce. A loved one who chooses to leave the relationship, and live differently, will also awaken many emotions within us. These emotions are very similar to the ones experienced when someone dies. That is why I will not only discuss the grieving process that one may experience after the death of a loved one but also the grieving process that one may experience with the loss of a loved one to a new life. When we lose a loved one in this way, there are often many feelings of bitterness, incomprehension, and anger in the person left behind which are much sharper and harder than similar feelings associated with the loss of a loved one to death. It is also more difficult to let go of the loved one who has not died, but lives elsewhere with a life of their own without us.

That is why it is often said that the grieving process takes a longer time when we lose a loved one to life rather than to death. But whatever loss we suffer, the grieving process will pass in broad lines along the same emotions, the same experiences, and that is why the description of the loss of a loved one through death is also the description of the loss of a loved one to a new life.

A feeling of insecurity

The death of a loved one is a shock that will influence our lives for years. In most cases this shock will work through the rest of the life of the person who is left behind. The shock will first deal with the realization of the supremacy of death: no one can hide from death. It will strike at random, but never when it suits us. That is very obvious. That is why the shock of the death of a loved one will awake in us the feeling of being unsafe. Nobody is safe. Whenever death wants to, it will strike and there is no one who can do anything to prevent this.

Of course, we know all this in our mind. We know that people die, but when death comes so close, the reality of death is so much more radical then we ever imagined. The death of a loved one destroys our feeling of safety and security in life. For years this feeling of insecurity will rear its head with regularity: it is possible that something will just happen to turn our life upside down. No one is safe since we are continuously threatened: our life is a threatened life. It will take a long, a very long, time for the person who is left behind to no longer feel the emotion of insecurity and to be able to face life with a certain faith.

> He was forty-five years old when he lost his wife to cancer. Both their children had only shortly before left home. One was married and the other lived in rented accommodation. In a very short time he was now completely on his own, where before he was part of a loving and warm family. Within 6 months he remarried, to a friend of his wife. This marriage had cooled the relationship with his children who saw this marriage as a betrayal of their mother.

For the man, however, this was a leap of faith although he would not admit to that. He could not face the loneliness. Five years after his second marriage I had a very good talk with him. During the conversation he said, "Security in life does not exist. You never know what can happen. Tomorrow everything can be different from what you thought." He said this as if he told a philosophical truth and did not realize how the emotion of insecurity, the fact that he had not dealt with the sorrow of the loss of his first wife and the cooled relationship with his children, all played a part. He did not want to talk about this, so he said, "There is no point in dragging all this up. It was all water under the bridge and what happened has happened."

Simply because he did not want to look back, the feeling of insecurity could continue for so long. If we do not live through those emotions to the bottom of our soul, and make them conscious in us instead of hiding them, then they will continue to work in us.

The fundamental feeling of insecurity – which originated through the death of a loved one – does do a lot to us. When you do not feel secure you are not in a position to give yourself in confidence to life and to the people around you. You become a withdrawn individual, and will never give yourself completely, but keep a wall around the most vulnerable parts of your heart. Those who are vulnerable are so easily hurt and moved, but those who are protecting themselves will be less surprised by the events life will throw at you. Someone going through the grieving process will therefore have to learn step by step to be open and unreserved for life and everyone around. Time is required for this process, lots of time and lots of love: love and warmth from people who are around the ones who are left behind. Only love and warmth can give us back our confidence, and only warmth and love can give us back the courage to be vulnerable again.

It is therefore entirely feasible that the man from the example above will heal from his feelings of insecurity through the love of his (second) wife. If she has the patience and love then she will be able break down the wall round the heart of her husband, and provide him with a new sense of security. Love is a greater force then awakening.

A spiritual quest

So many emotions are stirred when a loved one dies. Beside those feelings of insecurity we are also overwhelmed by feelings of fear. All sort of questions arise in a chaotic way without any connection. "How will life go on? Are we able to deal with everything coming at us? And what has to happen now?" Then there will be questions around the death of the love one: "What is death actually and how will our loved one go on? Is death the end or is there a life beyond death? Does heaven exist, and if so, where is it?" Of course, most of us have some ideas or thoughts about death. For one, death is the end of all life and for another, the deceased will go on to heaven or to hell, and for yet another group, death is the transition to a different, spiritual form of life. But however we think about this, at the time of the death of our loved one, it will become clear whether those thoughts and beliefs come from the heart, or are mere learned facts from our upbringing. It will occur to many people that the old answers do not stand up when death enters their lives. Those old answers appear to say nothing, and do not provide anything to hold on to, no insight and no consolation. They stand with empty hands and an empty heart, eye to eye with death. Many will experience this emptiness as unbearable. That is why they need answers, which they can feel within their heart. It has occurred to me that the death of a love one is often the starting point for a quest for answers about life and death – since the way we look at death will also determine the way we look at life. In this quest for answers many will arrive at a spiritual way of thinking, since only there do they appear to find the answers they are looking for and which can tell them what they want to know. They often enter a new world, a world that was previously unknown to them, but the desire to find answers to the questions of death will bring them there. You may say that the love for their loved one who died will bring them here. It is because they feel connected in love with the loved one that they want to know: where is the loved one now, what is her/his path beyond death, and how can we find reconnection with the loved one in our love for the deceased person? That is how the death of a loved one will bring us new challenges on our path, which we would not have discovered otherwise. In the book *Dealing with the Deceased*, which I co-wrote with Margarete van den Brink, I have given answers from the way the old, spiritual Christian tradition has dealt with questions about death.[1] And with a grateful heart I have been able to see that many found answers in those old traditions, answers for which their heart was longing, and they found comfort as their lives continued.

WHERE ARE YOU?

Your eyes are closed
Your lips rigid and cold
Your hands are folded
But you, where are you?

Your body cold and dead
Motionless without a move
It is you but at the same time
It isn't you at all
What was really you has gone
Your soul, your spirit
It isn't there at all

Where are you now?
I see you without speech
But I hear your voice
Your face a mask
But I see your smile
I see you are dead
But in my heart
You still live in full

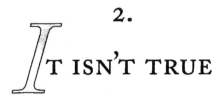

2.
*I*T ISN'T TRUE

A film camera

When a loved one dies it is so far-reaching that in the beginning what has actually happened does not sink in. This is in particular when our loved one dies unexpectedly, from a heart attack, needless violence, or a car accident. We do hear when we are told about the accident, or the crime that has been committed, or we see that the love one has had a heart attack, but for one reason or another it does not sink in. Our first reaction is often something like, "It cannot be true. It is only a bad dream."

But even if our loved one dies after a (short) illness, our first reaction is sometimes: it cannot be true that our beloved has died. Sure, we see that it is true. We see the lifeless body of our loved one, and yet we cannot fully comprehend. We expect – while we know that this is impossible – that our loved one will somehow get up, and start to smile, or that they will enter the room unexpectedly and will tell us that it was only a bad dream or a cruel joke.

We think that we can hear their voice at the most unexpected moment, and we stand still and listen, only to realize that the other person has died and cannot talk to us anymore. We hear the opening of a door and think: "There they are." We know in our mind that the other person has died and will never come through that door, but with our heart we cannot comprehend and understand. If we do sleep a little, then we wake up in the morning with a feeling that something terrible has happened, but what was it again? And immediately we realize what has happened, and at that moment the seriousness of the confusion, a feeling of powerlessness, sadness, and insecurity will come over us. It will take a while: that process of waking up and thinking "what has actually happened," and then immediately those dark emotions will engulf us like a tidal wave.

Only when death has come to set one free, when death comes after a long and terrible illness, can we greet death with a feeling of gratitude. Then we do not have those feelings of "it isn't true." On those occasions we have a feeling of inner silence, a certain peace (despite all the sadness), and we have a feeling of gratitude because an end has come to the painful suffering, something we could not shield our loved one from. You could say that in those situations a part of the grieving process has already been lived through during the illness of the loved one and that the stage of "it cannot be true" has been dealt with during that very long path of fear and sorrow that one went through.

But in most other cases it will occur to us during the grieving process: "I only dream this but it isn't real."

That first feeling of "it isn't true" can last a few hours, but also a few weeks. The emotion will cause a certain rigidity and make us feel like a machine. The way we do things and the way we act are mechanical. This attitude and rigidity often results in the fact that most people cannot cry during the funeral or cremation. They are not ready yet for emotions in this way, but are still in the stage of "it cannot be true." Others will often say, "They is very brave and strong." It has nothing to do with being brave and strong but with disbelief: "what is happening cannot be true..."

Together with that feeling of disbelief there will be a feeling of numbness. We observe everything around us even in minute detail. We see how people look at us, we see their confusion and their insecurity. We see the coffin, the color and the shape and we take these images in fine detail. We hear what is said during the funeral or cremation, and all those words we keep within our soul but, for one reason or another, the words do not penetrate to us. And what we see, all those images, we see as if we were a film camera. We do not feel anything with what we see. That is why we do not have any tears in the beginning: we are too bewildered and shocked and what has really happened cannot penetrate us. The feeling of seeing as a camera can last for quite a while. It means that in the first period after the death of the loved one we take in lots of well-defined pictures, just like a photo album. Later these pictures will re-emerge, and we will see them over and over again until finally we will feel some emotions with them. Only then the first tears will start to flow, and we will become aware of the depth of our loss and sorrow. But in the beginning this is just too much and all those feelings will be shut out.

Our soul is a wise entity in a certain way. It knows that we are not immediately able to feel and deal with everything from the word go, and that is why our soul will shut down our flow of emotions. The emotions are there, but they stay hidden in the depths of our soul. Only later will our soul allow these emotions to surface, so that we become aware of them. Only then, when our spiritual strength is sufficient to deal with the intensity of these emotions, can we feel them. In this we can see something of the silent inner guide, which I mentioned before.

Elisabeth Kubler-Ross tells us in her famous book *Teachings for the Living* about the various stages a dying person is going through. What happens to a person who has received the message that they haven't long to live and that no recovery is possible? The first stage according to Kubler-Ross is the stage of denial. The person has received the message that they haven't long to live but, for one reason or another, the message does not sink in. I had an experience in which I met someone who had just received the message that he had only two months to live, and then proceeded to tell me in a very enthusiastic fashion about the holiday he was planning with his family during the summer of next year in Venice. I remember very well that I listened in astonishment to his story, since I knew that he would not be there next summer, until it dawned on me that he really had heard the message his doctor had told him, but he simply denied it in his mind. This denial is an understandable reaction. Only when the individual involved has grown the strength to deal with such a drastic message will the soul allow it to enter our inner self. This stage of denial is therefore a certain protection from the soul to guard us from what we cannot deal with, and therefore it will be denied for a while.

A similar stage can be identified when a loved one dies. The stage of "it can't be true" is a stage where a certain amount of rigidity, lack of emotions, and acting like a machine can be displayed. So you can also call this stage one – which is similar to that which a dying person experiences – the stage of denial.

Why?

When the first feelings of rigidity start to break through then the first questions will also emerge and in particular the question of how this could happen. Has the doctor in the hospital paid attention to all details and not given the wrong treatment or has he misdiagnosed the patient? Did we not see that heart attack coming and if so could we not have prevented this terrible drama by taking precautions? Or, as we think to ourselves, we always said that our loved one was driving too fast. And then we ask ourselves why did they do it? Why did they not listen to us? The accident would have been prevented. The death of our loved one – in particular when it happens unexpectedly – is so difficult to understand that we are searching for explanations. There has to be a reason why this has happened. At this stage it is not possible for us to accept that there are no normal explanations for this. It appears that we can only accept it when we find a logical reason. And thus we will search for answers once the question of how this could happen enters our mind. It is a process in which the medical profession often takes the brunt of our questioning. They should have been able to spot if a heart attack was coming. They could and they should have been quicker and more accurate with their diagnosis. The illness could have been spotted earlier and therefore the death perhaps prevented. Each death is different, and therefore also the way we search for answers. But to search for a reason is the stage most people go through when the first feelings of being powerless and insecure are finally broken.

The quest for a reason appears to be an essential phase, since only later, when the person who is left behind has gone through this phase, does the moment come when they can accept within the soul, that whatever the reason was, it does not matter any more. It is an acceptance that the other person will never come back, and that one has to go on without the other person.

When people are going through the stage of searching for answers there is no point in other people defending, for instance, the medical profession (or whoever else gets the blame for the death of the loved one). It is always the person who is left behind who will have to see in time that the actual cause does not matter any more, simply because we cannot undo what has taken place.

Different, and much more difficult and painful, is the situation when there is a clear and obvious culprit. If someone has been murdered in a situation of senseless violence then it is understandable that all our anger and aggression is focused on the perpetrator. The inner struggle dominating the feelings of the person who is left behind is intense. It takes a long, long path of thinking, crying, emotions, and talking to yourself and others before one can leave the perpetrator for what they are. It is a path that eventually leads to the realization that what has happened, has happened. It cannot be undone, and there is only one way and that is the way forward, a path of loneliness without the other person. This path requires total attention and therefore emotions about the perpetrator must be left behind. But even then, the emotion of deep-seated anger toward the perpetrator is still within us and will surface, often after many years, to haunt us.

It often seems that our search for an answer as to the cause of death of our loved one is also an unconscious attempt to undo this death. Our quest for an answer is dominated by "what if": "What if my husband had left the house a little later, he would not have met the other car that killed him." Or "What if my wife had been diagnosed at an earlier stage by the doctors; she might have been saved." Or: "What if they had taken things easier, then the heart attack would not have come." What if, what if, what if... we search for scenarios and possibilities to undo the death of our loved one, to rewind the film in our mind. And we will continue to do this until we are so tired we realize that whatever we may think or do, it does not help us, it cannot be undone. We realize we have to accept the truth as it is.

This will not be achieved in an instant. It will progress with rattles and bumps along the way. We must allow the grieving person this slow process, and we should not try to stop it by providing logical answers, which only makes them feel more isolated. Because with all those "what ifs" the other person is only trying to say "I can't accept what has happened. I can't comprehend it at all. It is too severe that the other person will never come back." Behind all those comments on the "what if" scenarios, we can hear the despair. Those who can understand and hear this can also react with a reply, "What has happened is incomprehensible." With a remark like that, we do justice to the grieving and doubts of the other person. We have shown that we really do understand their powerless feelings.

This stage of "what if, what if, what if" is an integral part of the stage of denial. The "what if" comment is really an expression of inability to accept what has happened and is a (useless) attempt to undo what has happened.

Questions and decisions

In those first days a lot of questions and decisions will arise in the person who is left behind and a quick answer is required to some of them. What text is need for the death announcement? Is it a funeral or a cremation? What does it have to look like? Is there a church service and if so, where? Thankfully there are usually many friends and members of the family who can help with some of those tasks. For the person who is left behind, it is very important that they know that those tasks can be trusted to others. But they will still need to decide on many issues, even though their implementation can be trusted to others. Sometimes there are question like, "what about money?" If a man dies then it is important for the wife to know what the financial situation is going to be, and uncertainty about this may lead to worries. Some people may find that after the death of their loved one they cannot continue to live in the same house anymore simply because it may be too expensive, or it may have been a tied house. Others may ask themselves with despair "How will I be able to raise the children?" Such thoughts can be so oppressive that they can hardly accept them. Others are confronted with the fact that they have to empty the house and clear the belongings of the loved one – this may be so in the case of an elderly parent. There are all sorts of questions and problems which will arise and which through the fear, concerns, and insecurities will help break the initial shock. One has to act and think about the future.

What can others do?

What can others do to help in this stage for those who are left behind? The most important thing in the first few days is to have people around you who are not afraid of death, and who are capable of acting in a calm and dignified manner in this sad and difficult period. They are often people who have lost a loved one themselves, and have as a result lost their fear of death.

The bystanders do not need to say a lot. There is nothing to say. It is more important that they do what has to be done:

cooking, making tea or coffee for visitors, and assisting in organizing the funeral or cremation. But it is most important that they can do this from an inner peace, without fear. The person who is left behind will be overwhelmed by a chaos of thoughts, emotions, questions, and new experiences and it is therefore important that there are people who, with their inner peace, act as a beacon of trust, and are a pillar of strength to the person who is left behind.

They also require a fine-tuned sense of how to feel with the other person. They should not provide cheap, easy comfort during the grieving process: during that time there is no comfort only a little support.

A mother told me once about the funeral of her twelve-year-old daughter. It was almost five years ago, but for the mother it was still as if it was yesterday. She told me that a neighbor, during the condolences after the funeral, had said: "Never mind, you still have two other daughters." The mother remembered this precisely and when she spoke the words the neighbor had said, she became angry again. "Of course I have two other daughters. I know that, but that doesn't alter the fact that I longed, in desperation, for the one who was taken from me." That neighbor had hurt the woman deeply through her thoughtless words. The mother felt bereaved and so alone in her sadness, simply because the neighbor, with whom she had always been friendly, did not understand her feelings.

The best we can do – never mind how strange this may sound – is to admit in these situations that we haven't got any answers either, and that we do not know how to provide comfort. Only then does the other person feel understood in their despair. It is shared and it is this shared despair that provides a form of comfort.

> The journalist Louis Sinner reported for years on the experiences of cancer patients and in particular those with throat cancer. In later life he contracted throat cancer. Just before he died – through euthanasia – he was interviewed on television. During the interview he was asked what type of people had helped him during his disease. His reply was as follows: "The people who knew best, the know it alls, I detested, and I could really throw them out the room. But those who came into the room with a little hesitation and said: 'I don't know what to say' and who sat silent, sometimes with tears, beside my bed, those were the ones who helped me most. They provided comfort."

In particular, in the first stage after the death of a loved one, it is important that we have the courage to be empty handed, without answer, without comfort. The person whose mouth is empty in such a situation – who does not know what to say and feels helpless and powerless – they really share the suffering and despair of the other person. That person can provide a real comfort. This is a difficult, but also impressive, lesson in life: that we in our impotence, not through our replies, are able to provide comfort to the other person.

ON THE WAY

A last glance
A last sigh
Then you went

An empty shell
Your body
Dead and uninhabited
But you,
You are not here anymore
You entered a new world
A world without body
Where there is no heaviness
No pain and sadness

You were expected
Embraced and greeted
With radiance: since no
Human dies alone

You are beginning
On a new path
A new life full of light
Full of peace and love

I give you all my love
For you on your way
My heart is and stays
With you
Forever

3.

THE FIRST STEPS IN THE DARK TUNNEL

A stranger in a continuing world

The first period after the funeral or the cremation is often busy. Various people will come to visit or telephone. But sooner or later the phone calls become fewer, and there are not many visitors any more. The time has come when the person who is left behind faces him- or herself and has to experience the emotions within. The rush and the diversion of the phone calls and visits will die away, and the person who is left behind no longer has the opportunity to hide behind this diversion. For the first time they will come eye to eye with all the dark emotions that stir within.

Some have jobs and when they return to work some time after the funeral they will find a solace in the demands of their daily routine, or rather they find in the work a structure that saves them form drowning in the changing, chaotic, and dark emotions rising within.

Others have children who need them to make their food and

help them to school, etc. In this type of care too, no matter how difficult this is, they will find a certain solace.

This stage is most difficult for those who are alone, and who do not have such a daily rhythm or pattern (given through work or other responsibilities) to help them live from day to day. Because that is what it has become for those who are left behind: a life from day to day and they are unable to look beyond that one day. Waking up is still difficult. They still feel when they wake up the sense of "What has happened, what was it again?" And once reality has dawned upon them, they feel, "How will I get through the day?" It appears that from one day to another they have entered a dark tunnel where no light is visible. It is therefore good to have some responsibilities and duties from which you cannot walk away, even though you may want to do so very much, and even though it may be difficult to perform those duties to the best of your abilities. It gives strength during a period when all seems lost. Many have experienced their work or responsibilities to others as a godsend – and many say that without this they would not have been able to get through this dark period.

It also appears that life alone and with all these emotions is becoming more difficult rather then easier. It appears more and more apparent to the ones who are left behind what has actually happened, and it is this growing awareness of the inevitable truth that makes our lives darker, and more difficult, rather than easier.

For many it is incomprehensible that life just goes on. They sometimes read a little bit in the paper – they cannot yet do much more, because they have no inner attention or space for this – and it is strange to them that life just goes on as if nothing has happened. Their world has collapsed, but for the rest of the world it seems as if nothing has happened. The same applies to television. Always the same programs, the same newsreels just as if nothing has happened.

The person who is left behind feels like a stranger, as if they are no longer part of the common reality. All the inner attention is still so focused on what has happened, on the loved one who has died. That is why it is difficult to pay attention to all the trivial things other people talk about. What are all those things people talk about compared with the loss of a loved one? How can one be bothered with a new car, how can people be bothered about the weather? Does it matter whether the sun shines or if it rains? Why are politicians so bothered about things? And thus a rift emerges between the person who is left behind and the rest of the world. This rift is growing rather than getting smaller. This growing rift will make life increasingly more difficult rather then easier.

Many will not have a logical thought during this time. Inside they are in devastation, and all sorts of feelings and emotions bring chaos. The person who is left behind does not have a grip on this. Endless disconnected images emerge in a colorful fashion. Only the demands that life, work, and the people around you make, will prevent you from becoming crazy. That is how it feels anyway. A shadow appears to have fallen over one's life which forever – that is the way it appears – will taint everything with somber sadness. And you have the feeling that life will never be the same as it was before. That is how many live through the first period immediately after the loss of the loved one.

Warmth, human warmth, is dangerous for some. Others are looking for it, without ever finding it. There is no human warmth that can protect us from the darkness in ourselves, and from the coldness of the loss. That some people are afraid of warmth is connected with the fact that, as they say, they feel like crying if someone is nice to them: through the love that comes their way this pain and sorrow is accentuated. They don't want to cry, they want to be strong and try to live on in a '"normal" fashion. They are so afraid of the emotions of sadness in themselves; those feelings are so strong that they fear they will drown in them when they are touched by the warmth of someone else.

I think that what has been said here makes it understandable why many literally suffer from the cold during this time. It is as if they cannot become warm, as if the cold has penetrated them to their bones. Those who are afraid of warmth, because it makes them too vulnerable, or those who cannot find enough warmth to protect them against their sorrow, will experience the cold. Some may tell you that they experienced a deep-seated cold in bed and that they needed a hot water bottle or an electric blanket, even though it was high summer, just to keep warm. They also said that it took a long time before this feeling of being cold disappeared.

Meaningful memories

In those first moments memories will emerge – in particular, memories of the last few days or the last time before our loved one died. We hear the words again which they spoke, we see again how they looked upon us. And we try to listen and to look back to see if we can see or hear what was hidden behind those words and glances. Was there something in their words that sensed that death was near? Was there something in her/his eyes that betrayed a certain peace concerning what was about to happen? Did they know? And was there a silent message behind their words which we did not pick up but which we only now can hear? We talk about those last days or last times with people who visit us or to whom we speak over the telephone. During all those conversations we try to find the trail that had eluded us until now. It is strange that the people who are left behind often come to the conclusion that the deceased had known something – or rather, unconsciously felt something – about the coming departure, even if that departure came sudden and unexpectedly. It seems as if they finished their books before death came, though this would never have happened otherwise. As if there was a sense of foreboding, which gave the feeling that it was important to finish everything. Those signals, which we often only see and understand at a later stage, have mostly to do with clearing and tidying up; as if everything had to be cleared before the big journey beyond death could begin.

But looking back we can also detect messages in the remarks our loved one made to us. Maybe there was a chance discussion with our loved one just the week before, when they told us not to be sad if something should happen because we would always be connected. Or maybe by chance the other person thanked us for what we had meant in their life. Or... looking back there are so many words and gestures, so many glances that now appear important – full of a deeper meaning which we did not see before, but which in the light of what has happened are now more obvious. It is of course possible that we try to read too much into these memories, but it becomes clear that our deceased loved one must have known, or felt, something of what was about to happen. For some who are not used to this sense of foreboding (that people unconsciously know when they are about to die, even when death is unexpected) it may be difficult to accept. It can also be unacceptable to read a deeper meaning into these memories, words, and images.

When I was working as a pastor in a hospital I experienced, for example, that children always knew unconsciously if they would get better from their illness or if they would die. This was expressed in the drawings they made, in poems or fantasies that they wrote down, or in dreams that they shared. It was always correct! I learned from those children how strong the unconscious knowledge is within us, and how we are prepared for death in the depths of our soul even though death is not expected. I also discovered that this unconscious knowledge does live in adults as well as children. As a result of many of those experiences as well as the research that has been done in this area I am convinced that everyone knows, unconsciously, when they are about to die and this knowledge expresses itself in various forms. That is why it is not strange if those who are left behind can read deeper meanings in what was expressed at the time. In looking back to the period before death, the person who is left behind is more or less looking for evidence of this unconscious knowledge. It is strange but it provides comfort if one finds evidence of this unconscious knowledge. It is as if death becomes less of a mystery, less incomprehensible, and even appears to be logical from the unconscious knowledge of the deceased.

But if we look back to ourselves: did we also feel unconsciously what was about to happen and can we find that in our mind? I remember the last time I saw my brother before he died unexpectedly due to a heart attack. He stepped into the elevators and went down. Even though it is now more then thirty years ago,

I still see myself looking at him through the window of the elevator; I still see how he waved his hand; and I still feel what I felt back then: that this image for one reason or another was very important. Only because my soul knew, I stored this image razor sharp in all its detail in my mind. Later I was able to see unconscious knowledge in myself – or rather my soul – of this event. It still lives within me. Many people who are left behind look to their own memories to see if they can discover such foresight, such a suggestion of things to come. Of course, such emotions and experiences provide no form of evidence. And for bystanders they are often not very convincing. But for those who are concerned with this, those experiences say a lot, from a deeper level in the soul, because it shows that death did not come by accident, but by design in a greater plan, even though we do not understand this.

The way in which people who are left behind deal with these signals of unconscious knowledge varies a lot. Some believe that death is the end of everything, and they wonder about the signals that they also experience, but often they do not attach any value to them. Later, however, it can happen that these signals do have more influence, since the person who is left behind changes the way they think about death as a result of those signals. But this depends on the private views of life of each human being. To others, those signals are a sign – and in a certain way also the proof – of what they already knew: that death is not the end, but only a step into another dimension, another sphere of life. They see those signals as a sign from a greater world than the one that is accessible through our senses, one that can only speak to us from our inner mind and from the depths of our soul. The way people deal with these signals varies a lot, but the fact remains that the people who are left behind develop, during the grieving process, an inner sensitivity to those signals which emerge from their memories.

Two entirely different grieving processes

The way we deal with the loss of a loved one varies a lot. Some feel the need to talk about the loved one, to recall memories – sometimes from the desire to bring the other person back to life as if the other person is still there – even though there is always the painful conclusion that the other person is not there and will never come back in this life. It is a truth which will only slowly penetrate our soul: we still have the feeling that the other person might walk through the door or we see someone in the street who looks like the person we have lost, and in one single moment there is that thought as a flame of hope: there they are.

Other people – and often they are men, but not always – cannot talk at all about their deceased loved one. Talking means for them that emotions are stirred which they cannot deal with, and therefore they avoid such conversations. They deal with their sorrow on their own in the hidden depths of their soul. They find a way to deal with their sorrow and to place it within themselves, sometimes in the tranquility of nature, through walking or fishing, or in music, in writing poetry or texts, or even in painting. There is no point in telling them that it is better to talk about their loss, because talking will provide a release. It does not release them, and it makes them so very emotional that they become afraid of their own feelings. Everyone reacts to a loss in the same way as they have always done to difficulties or problems. We have developed our own way of dealing with things, and one way is in principal not better than another. Personally I do not feel the need to judge this, and say that someone who talks will deal with the grieving better then someone who grieves in silence, without much talking at all. It becomes risky and more alarming when someone is continuously on the run, constantly busy to avoid their own emotions. This does not need to be serious at first, but when it becomes a permanent situation, and there is no peace except in hard work and being busy, then the person runs the danger of becoming stuck in the grieving process to the extent that they become estranged from themselves.

The different pattern of dealing with emotions can be difficult, for example when a couple loses a child and the mother wants to talk, and the father doesn't. Then they cannot provide each other with support during their sorrow; quite the contrary. The mother feels abandoned by her husband, and feels stuck, because when he is there, she cannot talk about their beloved child who has died. The husband feels alone because his wife does not seek any diversion with him, and is not in tune with him, burying himself in work. It is not accidental that after the death of a child the likelihood of divorce shoots up. A marriage can only stand such a difference in dealing with the loss if there are true bonds, real love, and respect between the parents, which are stronger than the feelings of loneliness and abandonment during the grieving process.

Often the mother will want to talk a lot and the father doesn't, but we cannot say that this is typically male or female, since the reverse can also take place. It depends on the character and the past history of every person as to how they live through the grieving process.

The first emotions become noticeable

The first period after the funeral or the cremation, the period that I mentioned as the "first steps in the dark tunnel," is the stage where the initial rigidity and feelings of being numb are beginning to break through, and all kinds of emotions become noticeable. Despair, fear for the future, a deep painful feeling of emptiness and sadness, a feeling of loneliness, the feeling of being a stranger among other people for whom the world continues to go on as if nothing has happened, feelings of guilt, anger – everything will surface in an odd mixture of strange and incomprehensible feelings. Each day these feelings are there. And each day you have to face these feelings again.

Sometimes I compare it to a drill at the dentist's: the drill will mill round and round your tooth. But with each turn the drill will enter deeper into the tooth until it hits the nerve (thankfully we have such things as injections at the dentist). That's how it will happen with this mixture of emotions, which will emerge during the first stages of the grieving process: every day they are the same feelings, it is the same mixture and chaos, but it appears as if the feelings become stronger and are harder to bear. And as we get ever closer to the naked truth – our loved one has died and nothing can undo this situation – we have to accept it whether we want it or not. In this way each time we take another step into that dark tunnel. And we can hardly imagine that there is an end to that tunnel. It is rather as if the further we go the less we can imagine that there will ever be light and an end to this.

The clothes of our loved one

In the first period the clothes of our loved one still hang in the wardrobe. Their bed is still in their room and we find very personal thing gathered around it, that they collected.

There are people who smell the clothes of their loved one. But this scent can bring about so much sadness, that their sorrow and the feeling of being alone will only grow stronger. Some say that they find themselves with personal items belonging to their loved one in their hand and then suddenly remember why they bought that, and why they were attached to it.

Some people, almost immediately after the funeral or the cremation, will clear out all the personal items of their loved one. It brings too much pain to be confronted with them all the time, and it does not help their sorrow to have all those items around. Others want to keep all those items as long as possible, to have something real from their loved one. One way is not better than the other, but it is important to listen to what our heart tells us.

What can bystanders do in this phase?

It is important that the bystanders have an understanding of the process the person who is left behind will go through, and of the fact that it will only get more difficult rather then easier. They can support the other person by being prepared to listen to the stories the person wants to tell them. They can help by being prepared to listen to those stories over and over again, even though they know them by heart. Vroman tells us this in a well-known poem about the war: "Come tonight with stories, how the war has ended, and repeat them a hundred times. Every time I will cry." Stories about far-reaching events have to be told many times over, and each time it will stay important to tell those stories, since only then the reality will penetrate through us. Only in this way can the person who is left behind become aware that it is a goodbye, and not a bad dream. Through talking and through repeating those stories the person can become aware of the new reality. In addition the stories which initially only dealt with memories of the deceased will get a new function: initially they were meant to recall the deceased back into reality, but slowly the aspect of awareness of the unique being of the deceased will emerge: who were they in reality?

What were their ideals? What were their special and unique qualities? What have they meant for other people? What have they left on this earth in their own special way? All those questions will be put in the light of the growing and clear sense of who she or he really was. Bystanders can help in this process by recalling their own stories about the deceased, and by helping to search for the special and personal meaning the loved one had.

We can help those who do not want to talk in a different way. Very simply by showing small signs of cordiality and sympathy. Everyone can imagine what small gifts can display a sign of sympathy. Bystanders must realize that it is nice if they can continue this for a while even though the other person hardly seems to, or does not, react to those niceties. They find it difficult to react because they have hidden their emotions and can do nothing else. They can therefore not react to nice things, but they mean a lot to them.

Most important for bystanders is that they do not try to console too early, or provide a type of consolation that the other person cannot use – no matter how true what they say may be. You could say, for instance, that the deceased person has been spared a lot of sorrow and problems. But such a remark can raise anger and resistance in the person who is left behind in the way of: "That may be true, but I them, and it is painful that I don't have them around me anymore. Don't you understand that?" Often it won't be said but is very often thought! It is important for bystanders to listen to the person first, and try to feel what is going on inside them – only then can you say things that are connected to what the other person experiences inside. A wise person says only the things that are connected with the inner feelings of the other person, and will limit himself to that. Pious remarks can also fall on deaf ears at this stage. For example: "The other person now lives with God and lives in the light." That may be a hundred times true (and for myself it is even the deepest truth), and yet it can sound like a curse at that stage. Since now, at this stage, the emphasis lies on pain and a missing feeling, there is no space to think about the path that our loved one who has died has started beyond death. Only when this knowledge begins to emerge in the one left behind, and when they begin to talk about it, only then can we confirm this thought as our innermost deepest conviction. But not before the other person has really opened up to this.

THE JOURNEY

So strange
My heart can follow
You a bit
On your journey

In the beginning,
The first few days
You were very close

I heard you talking
I saw you walking
Later you floated
Further away from me
And it became
More difficult
To follow you

I feel:
You travel further still
Away from me
You travel toward
The highest light
I feel the growing distance
And that hurts
But I know
The further you go
The more radiant the light
How intense the peace
How stronger the love

Go and go with God
That is my highest
And deepest wish

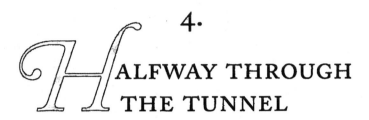

4.

HALFWAY THROUGH THE TUNNEL

Depression

The dark tunnel: the further you go into this, the more you think there is no future, at least not one you can see or believe in. You feel dominated only by sorrow, through the sense of missing, and all those changing emotions of intense loneliness, rebellion, the questions of why, and the feeling of being outside society. There is only the past, to which you look back, and of which you increasingly become aware that it is a past that will never come back. You are only focused on the past, and there is no future as yet – that is how you can summarize this dark period. In this situation you cannot do much more then try to keep going in the dark – with the fearful question in your heart: will there ever be light at the end of the tunnel? Will you ever feel some form of happiness? You cannot imagine that now, but maybe, just maybe, it is meant for you.

Those who feel the need to talk a lot about the lost loved one will sooner or later become aware that all that talking does not actually help them. They become increasingly aware that those to whom they speak about their loved one do not really understand, and are not able to feel how much pain this missing feeling really is. An when they realize this, they start to feel more depressed after such a conversation, as if that conversation has highlighted their loneliness rather then made it easier. It can hurt if you talk with someone else about the deepest experiences and emotions of your life and you feel that what you are trying to say does not penetrate to the other person. In such a moment you will feel very much alone. That is why most people, sooner or later, will stop talking about their loved one and the feeling of something missing and become more isolated within themselves. For some it can take up to two years before the talking gradually stops and they turn into themselves, while others take a much shorter time. But it is something that many people will recognize as the way it has happened in their lives.

At this point, halfway through the tunnel, the feeling of loneliness becomes stronger. You become aware that talking does not help any more and that you are alone with all those feelings within you and that people around you don't understand. You become shy, and even afraid of people, since you are not interested in what they are doing, and what is uppermost in your heart becomes increasingly difficult to talk about. You question the meaning of life for yourself and thoughts of suicide are not uncommon. Significantly, however, the rate of suicide does not increase after the loss of a loved one. Research does, however, show that the death rate among widowers during the first six months of the death of their wife is higher. There are approximately 40 per cent more deaths among widowers then the statistical average would indicate. That is a significant increase. It appears that these men become depressed through the loss of their wife, become more reckless, and do not care. It does not matter to them what happens. They do not cling to life, and as a result of their sorrow, they often long secretly for death and they will therefore die earlier.

The period in the middle of the dark tunnel is in fact a most depressed one. Oddly, most will see later how depressed they really were, but at the time they were not aware of it. Maybe this is also a form of self-preservation: if you realize how depressed you really are then the chances are that the depression will take over, rather then you seeing it as a phase to a, hopefully, better and different life. Most people will only admit much later to themselves that, when they were in this darkest part of the process, they were on the verge of self-destruction. When it happened they had their hands full, in order to survive from day to day. Only later can they see this as part of the bigger picture and see what the reality was. I have often heard people talking, with amazement in their voices, about the time in the middle of the dark tunnel, and how they felt so depressed that they were really at the point of no return.

Feelings of guilt

Of course those thoughts will go back, and back again, to the loved one who died. Initially the thoughts and memories will circle around the last period on earth. The questions are constantly how this could have happened, why everything went as it did, and also there is a searching for what went wrong during those days. Later, the memories will go back further and feelings of guilt will emerge. Various images will return to the memory – and with them the questions that we ask ourselves when we see these images. Why did I react the way I did? Why did I hurt him/her at that time? Because we cannot make good – at least that is the way we experience this – our shortcomings with the loved one are accentuated. These feelings of guilt will play games with us, and will keep us occupied for a long time. If you can speak about these feeling at all with others, their replies won't help you: most people react with the words that you could not have reacted in any other way and they will do their very best to talk you out of these feelings of guilt. But they cannot be dismissed that easily, and that is why we can suffer this for a long time, despite what other people say. We, as bystanders, will have to take these feelings of guilt seriously, and we shouldn't try to talk them away so easily. Because it is true: what has happened has happened and it cannot be undone, ever. We cannot ask the other person for forgiveness.

For people who have an inner connection with God there is the possibility of bringing these feelings of guilt before God in prayer and asking for forgiveness. This is only possible when you have lived through your feelings of guilt to the bottom of your heart. Only then, when you cannot take it any further, can you bring this before God in prayer and release this guilt into his hands in order to stop it. For people who do not have an inner connection with God, it will be much more difficult. With them, you can see that these feelings of guilt and shortcomings are hidden within their souls and will emerge with certain regularity.

With these feelings of guilt it is often the case that we want to see the loved one who has died in a better light then they really were. "Never speak ill of the dead" as the saying goes, and that is how we often act and react. We find it difficult to acknowledge that the other person was not a saint and also had their faults. We are inclined to look at ourselves first for all the reasons why things went wrong. As long as we have a one-sided view of the other person, our feelings of guilt will also weigh heavily on our soul and mind. Only when we allow ourselves to see the loved one as they really were, can these one-sided views of guilt be set aside, and we can see the shortcomings in our relationship to which we were both guilty parties.

There we hit on another important fact within the grieving process: how important it is to see our loved one as they were when they were alive, rather than our rose-tinted view of them, as a being with beautiful and loving attributes but also as a flawed being with their problematic side. The process of seeing ourselves, as well as the other person, as we really were is not easy. It requires honesty: not to make us darker or to see the ugly side but not to make us prettier either. We need to look at our loved one with the same honesty and see who they really were. This is an important part of the grieving process.

Others can help us with this part of the process. We can ask them how they viewed and experienced our loved one, and hope that they want to tell us in an honest way. If this can happen in a loving manner then both the positive and the negative side of our loved one can be discussed. Such honest conversations can help us to see ourselves and our loved one in a clear and pure light. We see then that the grieving process is, in a way, a process of awareness to gain insight into the other person and ourselves. This process on its own is very important to us. It can help us to let go of these feelings of guilt. It can help us to see how the other person really was, and the more we are able to see this the more we are able to let go of them. It also helps to gain insight into our own soul. It is therefore very important that we focus on this process with all our love and courage to gain clear insight, and that we take all the time we need. This process will take years for some, rather than months.

This process is also important for another reason. In my opinion our deceased loved one will undergo a similar process of awareness in the spiritual world. I have written about this on previous occasions. If this is true – and I am personally convinced of it – than it is important that the process of becoming aware will run simultaneously for both the loved one who died, and for the one who remains on earth. We come together, one on earth and the other in the spiritual world, to awareness and insight in our deepest selves. Our awakening here on earth will work through to the spiritual world, and will act in a stimulating way on the process of awakening our deceased loved one. Vice versa, the processes that are experienced by our loved one will work on us here on earth. In other words, if we work with love and honesty to gain insight into the true nature of our relationship here on earth, and to see the other person and ourselves as we really are, than that same process will be a stimulant for our deceased loved one in the spiritual world. That is why it is so important to begin with this process. It is really special to realize that, now your beloved has died and lives on in the spiritual world, you can still help and support them in this way. You begin to realize as well that the bond of love will remain and does not disappear with death. This bond will only transform into another form because it is now only a spiritual bond.

It may sound strange to those who are not used to this type of insight. But we can imagine how the new and different connection may work. Imagine you have a dispute with someone, or there are other types of problems which have not been resolved through talking, and that the relationship has cooled down as a result of this.

How great would it be if you could talk about those issues with the other person! When you realize that the other person is open and prepared, just like you, to look in honesty to their part in the dispute, then the problems will disappear in no time, and with it the coolness in the relationship.

But if the other person is not prepared to listen and talk in frankness and honesty, but continues to say, "It is all your fault" then you will stay for a long time with these terrible feelings. You will be stuck for a long time in this conflict. Thus we can see how important it is to be able to discuss things together. It works the same way when a deceased loved one and the person who is left behind are working each in their own way and in their own world one on earth and the other in the spiritual world – toward insight and awareness; if they speak to one another in an honest and open way about what was never said. This is really possible: that we can still say what we want to say; that we speak about our shortcomings to the other person; and that we speak about the issues in which we felt wronged by the other person.

We can do this in a simple ritual. We can write a letter to our deceased loved one in which we can express ourselves very carefully in all we want to say. If we can do that without reproach, but with love and understanding, and then read that letter to the other person, something real is happening. You may invite someone who you can trust to take part in that ritual. You can put down a photograph of the loved one, light a candle, and say a prayer and read the letter out loud. You can ask for forgiveness and also tell the other person what you want to forgive. You can then close the ritual with another prayer or a text you both loved and blow out the candle. You will see how much relief this will bring to the soul. It is as if a real reconciliation has taken place, and as if you can really be close again and this is true in a spiritual sense.

What is really touching is that through this form of assistance to the deceased loved one and also to yourself, you become aware at the same time in the new way that you and your loved one will be connected. The more you become aware of this new, different kind of connection, the more the middle of the dark tunnel will become brighter with the first glimpse of light in the dark.

The quest

The quest for the meaning of death will start for many in the darkest depths of this tunnel. I have mentioned this already, since this search started at an earlier phase. But, now we have progressed in the tunnel, the need for the quest increases. We need answers with which we can live and are prepared to use all the power in our soul to really find those answers – answers that will convince us in our innermost self, and with which our soul can be at peace. The search will start with the fact that we cannot imagine that we will never see each other again.

All the feelings in our heart resist this idea. We cannot imagine that there is no connection with our loved one, and that death really means the end of everything. But if death is not the end, what is death? Does heaven exist, or hell? These questions are fed by the fact that some still feel a connection with the deceased, for instance in dreams.

> She dreamt she was lying in a bed. Suddenly her husband was beside her in bed. He wore the nice suit she had bought for him just before he died. Smiling he

said, "You were right. Life continues beyond death." He looked a bit shy, as if he felt caught. In her dream she knew immediately why. During his life he did not want to know about life after death. Dead was dead for him. Then he said, "I feel very good here, I am happy." He looked at her again. In his look she read his lasting love for her. Then his appearance began to fade, and she woke up. This time she had a happy feeling while normally she would wake up feeling sad.

For this woman, her meeting with her husband in her dream was lifelike and experienced as a real meeting. For her it was more then a dream. It was, in one way or another, the expression of a deeper level of reality. That is how she experienced it. That is why this dream was for her a sign that she was right and death was not the end, but a new beginning. She received this dream in the middle of her tunnel, but it was a deciding turning point in her grieving process. She was now able to walk toward the end of the tunnel toward the light.

Many receive a sign from the deceased loved one. Most often subtle signs, but yet they are signs. Some say that the image of the photograph of their loved one suddenly changes and begins to radiate. This is a change that is not imaginary, but real, and which has been experienced by many as they have told me independently from each other. Others tell me that they could suddenly smell the aftershave from their husband or the perfume of their wife in their house or bedroom or kitchen. They could smell it very clearly, and it would linger for hours, while nobody had been in the house with that particular perfume or aftershave. In this smell they experienced a real presence of their loved one. Others hear an inner voice: the voice of their loved one which sounds so clear that they don't know if it is coming from inside or outside. A voice that gives a short message like, "Don't be sad, I am very happy." Or "Do not worry, I will look after you." Or "Mummy, I am with you and will help you." Of course, most people who experience this are deeply touched and also bewildered. In our culture we are not used to the fact that the dead can speak to us. But everyone who has told me about such a voice was convinced that this was really the voice of the loved one, and that they had not made this up or brought it on out of desire. However, most of them did also indicate that they did not speak about this with others because they were afraid that they would not be taken seriously, while this experience was precious to them.

In our time there are many ways to experience a connection with our loved ones. There are people who tell me that their loved one just appeared to them while they were fully conscious, and that they were suddenly in their room and gave them a message. There are more people who do receive signs of "life" from their deceased loved ones, than there are who don't, as determined by American research. It says a lot about the measure of these experiences even though little is said about them. I was allowed to see my brother up to three times after his death.

> Unexpectedly he stood in the room, surrounded by a beautiful light. The last time he appeared – which was about one year after his death – he showed me his right hand with a golden ring on his middle finger. Then he said, "This is the last time that I will come here; now I go for good." I was wide awake and fully aware all three

times he appeared. Later I felt that the ring round his middle finger was a sign of healing. He was now the human being that he had always been in his deepest being, and now he was ready to move on to the higher world of light. His visits meant for me that I changed my way of thinking about death. Besides, the warmth of the light that surrounded him when he appeared still warms me to this day when I think about it.

Those experiences, such signs of life which we receive in one way or another from our deceased loved one, will influence our way of thinking about death: what is death? Does one live on beyond death? Is death only a different form of life, a life in a different dimension from our earthly dimension?

I would like to emphasize that such life signs of our deceased loved ones require an open mind, in which our thinking does not get the chance to destroy what we experience, which sometimes happens in our society. How often does it happen, when we experience or feel something, that we say to ourselves, "We only imagined it." Those who are stuck in this way of thinking will receive many sign of "life" from the deceased loved one but will destroy them by thinking. It is very easy to destroy them since the signs are very subtle. They are spiritual signs and not material ones.

Sometimes I meet people who tell me that they would love to receive a sign of life from their loved one in the same way as other people do, but that they have never received such a sign. But when we continue the conversation they will say that, for example, they sat in their room one evening feeling sorry for themselves, and suddenly they felt a soft touch on their shoulder, as if someone very carefully

placed a hand on their shoulder. At the moment they felt in that touch the presence of their loved one and felt comforted for a moment. But later they asked themselves, "Did it really happen or did I imagine it?" And soon their thinking will get the upper hand of their feelings and they will conclude that it was only their imagination because such a touch is simply not possible. When they tell me that, and when I explain that the touch was the way the loved one made the connection, they suddenly understand, and accept the gift they had been given and which they had put aside.

Again and again, when we receive such a life sign, the process of thinking and reflection about death will start. Many will consume a number of books about the subject in a short space of time. One book will have something to say while another doesn't. It doesn't matter. But from all the reading an answer will emerge in their mind about the question of death.

To their amazement, some will start reading books that they would never have read before the death of the loved one. Through the painful experience of loss they will enter a whole new world of experiences, and begin to question many different things. A whole new world opens up for those who are left behind after the period of reflection.

In the middle of the dark tunnel this process of change will start, so that when we finally emerge from the tunnel we become different beings from who we were before our loved one died.

LOVE IS EVERLASTING

I know: there is a world
Beyond the borders of death

I know: beyond the darkness
Of death awaits the light

Don't ask me how
I know, I just know
With my heart
I can hardly believe
But yet my heart is
Sure of it: death
Is not the end
It is only a new beginning

Now I know that my beloved is alive
Even though his body is dead
His earthly life finished
But he began
A new life full of
Light and love, full of peace

I know: love is everlasting
Love cannot die
And that is why we remain
Connected in everlasting love
And when I too will reach
The frontier of death
We will see each other again

Because love is everlasting
And will keep us connected
Now and forever

5.

$\mathscr{A}$LL THOSE EMOTIONS...

Anger

As time goes on, emotions will grow stronger – at least if we don't deny them. The temptation for this is great. Emotions are often so severe that we are sometimes afraid that we will be overwhelmed by them. "Once I start crying or screaming I won't stop and I will drown in this," someone said. With this he put in words what many feel, and why they are inclined to keep emotions under control.

Thankfully it is often time itself that makes the wall, which we have built around our emotions, crumble.

Feelings will then get the chance to emerge, step by step, which is just as well, because as long as the wall is there we will never heal, never become our real self, and never really warm inside. If we close off our emotions, and thus our feelings, than we also close off the warmth others would like to give us. But when they finally break through, then all the emotions of anger and abandonment are difficult to deal with. Sorrow we will allow, although not always, but anger? That anger is particularly there if our loved one has ended their life by choice. While we may be able to understand why the

71

other person decided to do this, and why life was unbearable, we will feel intensely sad about it, and quite apart from our feelings of understanding are other feelings as well. Those feelings are dominated by hurt and anger, since our loved one's action was deemed to be selfish, with no thought for us. It is important to allow ourselves this anger, and the emotions that result from being left alone, and then to realize that our anger is also a sign of love. Because if you don't care for someone, you cannot be angry with that person either; you would be indifferent.

It is strange, however, that those emotions can overwhelm us suddenly from one minute to the next. They can, just as quickly, disappear again, or change into something else, like sadness. This whole range of changing emotions is very typical of the grieving process.

Anger does not occur solely with suicides, but in one way or another is part of any grieving process. The reason for this is that (from a spiritual viewpoint), when coping with a severe loss, we always revert to the position of a child. When we lose our spiritual maturity we go back into a childlike phase. A child knows anger when it is left on its own, even though there may be lots of reasons why this should be so. For a child those reasons are not important: the only thing that counts is the fact that they are left alone. We all react a little like that child when we lose someone we love. In loss, we fall back into childlike thinking and we feel angry. It is very important to acknowledge these feelings and allow them to be released in ourselves instead of repressing them. Because this happens easily, we tell ourselves that it is not fair to be angry, or to feel abandoned, since the other person could not help it. And in the blink of eye, the feelings of anger and abandonment have gone. But they are not really gone; they are only pushed into one corner of our soul, where they continue to grow. Eventually they will emerge in a distorted manner, for example when we are angry at politicians, or the behavior of young people, or whatever is the target of the moment.

But we will never lose our anger in this way. To get rid of these emotions it is far better to say to yourself that you just feel it that way. It makes much more sense to feel these emotions of anger and abandonment to the very bottom and then let go. We can only let go of feelings when we have felt and lived through them. That is the secret of letting go.

She was thirty-five years of age and had lost her husband three years ago. He had suddenly died of a heart attack. During the conversation she said: "Strange, they say that during the grieving process you also experience feelings of anger. Well I have not felt this at all." A bit later she told me that she sometimes felt anger toward her children, which she felt was unreasonable. When I asked her if she had noticed that this occurred more often she replied, "Yes, since you ask me, I believe that that is true. I also feel that I am angry with others as well. I only learn to control it and keep it inside me." Before her husband died she did not have those feelings, those attacks of unreasonable anger. Slowly it dawned on her that those feelings of anger, which are part of the grieving process, manifested in her as unreasonable anger toward others. Once she had understood this, the attacks lost their power and gradually disappeared. Recognition and becoming aware of them destroyed those feelings.

But beside feelings of childlike anger there are sometimes other types of feelings of anger.

This emerges from what we experienced with the other person. Because we are human there may be, beside all the nice and pleasant experiences together, a number of painful things as well, which we never talked through. Almost every relationship knows those moments. That is normal. But now, looking back, when the memories re-emerge, those unspoken and unprocessed experiences and emotions surface as anger. It is important that you allow yourself those feelings and watch them closely. They make clear to us what has to be put straight between us and the other person. I have explained in the previous chapter how this could be done. We have a tendency to suppress our emotions almost immediately. It is not nice to be angry with our deceased loved one. If we deal with our feelings in this way we make a mistake. We forget that those feelings are in reality a gift, because they indicate what has not been dealt with properly between ourselves and our loved one, and what stands between us in a spiritual way. Only when we take these feelings seriously can we work with them. We can become more aware of how the relationship really was. And with this realization we can help both ourselves and the other person.

All those changing emotions, which seem to overwhelm us at the beginning of the grieving process, are one huge chaos. We don't have a grip on them but we feel we are being tossed in the wind. It makes life difficult. One day you feel reasonably good, while the next day you feel rotten and hopeless. Those feelings and emotions change by the hour, even faster sometimes. One moment you feel not too bad, and the next black and dark. Many people will tell you that they find it difficult to make appointments during this period. They never know how they will feel until the moment of the appointment, and are unsure whether or not they can cope with what they are going to meet. And thus they leave things to the actual day and see how they feel, whether or not they can have dinner with someone, for instance, or go to the shops with someone else. You can read from this example how emotions during the grieving process can rule our lives rather than the other way round. It usually takes a long time before we get a grip on our emotions so that they no longer rule our lives.

Beginning of order

In the chaos of emotions some order will slowly appear. We begin to understand and discern it bit by bit. For instance, there are emotions in us that are wholly focused on the other person: the sorrow for the other person's path to their death. If a long and painful illness was the prelude to our loved one dying, then it is possible and understandable that we feel a long period of sadness about this agony. If it was a child who died than we will feel sadness for a long time for the young life that was cut short. And even if some of those who are left behind are beginning to understand that no other way was possible, and they might even understand that the child themselves might have chosen this short life, it can still hurt that a promising life was cut short before its time. As human beings we know so many different and opposite feelings and emotions at the same time. That is why it is possible that, beside a growing understanding for this unique and short life path of the child, it is also possible that the pain is still there because the life was cut short so early.

Her only son was nineteen years old when he died in a car accident. She felt torn apart in the deepest part of her soul. "This is far worse than the divorce from my husband ten years ago," she said. She took care of the funeral arrangements, and was than left alone with her sorrow, questions, and despair. She began to read all kinds of books about death. She had to know. What is death? She read about karma and reincarnation; she read about the spiritual world and how deceased people would live on, according to various authors. Through all those books and all she was able to think about, it dawned on her that her son, before he began this life on earth, had chosen this short life. It gave her peace in a certain way. "The pain is not any less," she said, "but I can understand now why it has been this way." She had had an upbringing with a traditional belief and those new insights created a rift with the past. "But," she said, "I actually knew those things in my heart. It is as if I find something which already lived in me but I was unaware." Some people thought that she embraced those new insights because there was no other way to live with the death of her son. "Of course I need an answer," she said to that, "I have to know where he is and how he is. But this is not an answer of the mind, but one that provides peace in my heart. And this peace which arises from my sorrow, is the greatest gift I have ever received, even though it is a difficult present."

Beside searching for answers to the many questions, and beside the sadness and feelings which are mainly focused on the lost loved one, there are also emotions about ourselves in this dark period. Sorrow because we are suddenly alone. Or sorrow because we have to miss the warmth and tenderness of the other person, and we now feel cold and chilled in our life. Or fear, which comes from the fact that we don't know if we really can live on without the direct support of the other person. The further we come, the more we learn to distinguish all those different emotions, and recognize them. This rearrangement process is the start of, step by step, getting a grip on our emotions so that we do not feel tossed in all directions.

The further we go, the more we learn to feel those emotions at the same time, for instance the heaviness of the sorrow, and beside this we can give attention to something or someone else. This was not possible in the beginning when our emotions overwhelmed us. But now, since there is a little order in everything, and we can recognize, understand and deal with our emotions a little better, we can also begin to pay attention to other things and other people. That is not always easy. When we are alone again we often feel that we have accomplished a difficult task, and we are relieved to be alone again. But still, the fact that we are able to pay attention to someone else, means a step forward. Slowly a little clarity begins to emerge where before there was only chaos.

(Over) sensitivity

Some people may know this. They have the flu, and with the flu comes a certain over-sensitivity, which they normally do not have, for instance, to sounds. A creaking door can really hurt you deep in your soul. Loud voices can make you shrink. It is as if you are wrapped in cotton wool and live a different, more sensitive, level of consciousness. The same can happen to us when we have a pain in the soul. A strong feeling of sorrow may be called a pain of the soul, even though this may be too weak an expression for the present time we live in. At such times we also become more sensitive than we normally are. It is as if we feel more intensely than ever what others think, or we know what others will say to us before they have opened their mouth. Sometimes we know already who has called before we pick up the phone. It is as if the borders of perception have shifted, and that the limitations of matter are no longer valid. It is also as if we become more sensitive to greater dimensions, which appear to be closed to us in normal life.

Not everyone has this sensitivity during the grieving process. It depends on many different things, in particular on your own way of life. If you have always been a person who uses the mind, the thinking process, to meet all questions and problems you will encounter in life, then you will do the same when confronted with the grieving process. Thinking in particular can get in the way of increased sensitivity. If you are such a person then you will not notice much of this increased sensitivity during the grieving process. But others with a different approach to life will experience it much more.

This increased sensitivity will allow us something special: it is possible to follow the path beyond death of our deceased loved one. We feel the presence of our loved one during the first few days after the actual time of death. It is very hard to describe how we feel this. It is part of our increased sensitivity, which enables us to sense those dimensions and a world that is normally closed to us. We feel especially the presence of our loved one, and this feeling goes with a sense of security, which no one can take away from us. We also sense that after about three days our loved one will be further away from us and cannot be followed so directly. Their presence is less clear and less defined. Thanks to this sensitivity we can follow the path of our loved one, and feel a little of where they are going.

It is a pity that most of us have not learned to trust this sensitivity, and therefore do not pay attention to what it is trying to tell us about the path of our loved one on the other side. But those who do, and who can appreciate the journey of the loved one on the other side of death, will also experience comfort and consolation in this fact. Because we do feel how our loved one will make this journey, step by step, until the point that we cannot follow them any further, and our sensitivity can no longer detect their presence, we can go with them until they have reached the higher light spheres, which we are not able to experience.

But this sensitivity has another aspect. You will begin to appreciate how much help will come from greater dimensions to assist us in the difficult times. People often reflect and say how much they felt help and assistance in those difficult times. Looking back they see that nothing happened by coincidence, but that at the right moment the right person, whom they needed, called. Or that at the right moment they received the right book, which helped them to understand the issues they were struggling with. Or they experience, as they say sometimes, that they sit all alone one evening in their house and feel the presence of something warm, silent, and comforting. And that while they felt so hopeless a few moments before! What kind of presence was this? Who was this being? An Angel? Christ? Who it is they often don't know, but they felt with their whole hearts how comfort and consolation was brought to them from a greater world than this.

When you are in the midst of the grieving process, you do not yet know how much you receive in help and guidance. Only later when you feel the inner peace and quiet again, you realize from this inner silence, what you discovered in the chaos of all those emotions: help and guidance. The discovery of this help and guidance will make people look at life in a different way. Because now they know that a human being does not go alone through the dark, but will be carried through it in the most wonderful way. It is that knowledge that will provide them with the confidence to live with a new and greater devotion. A new inner benefit is born from the depth of all sorrow. I would like to emphasize, for those who have experienced this, that this benefit will only emerge to us in a tangible form later. When we are still in the dark we don't notice anything of this guidance and help. That is why it is wrong to say to someone who is still in the dark that guidance is there to help them. At that moment they will feel nothing, but will only experience the intense emotions which are moving in him or her, and which are difficult to survive.

Escape in drugs

The emotions are sometimes so severe that quite a few people will look at the possibilities for escaping from the pressure of those feelings. Apart from work, people often escape in drink. Because alcohol is a suppressant of our emotions, most people feel a bit better after the consumption of a few glasses of alcohol. Unfortunately alcohol only works for a short time, and the emotion will return in full strength the next morning. Besides, it appears that increasingly larger amounts of alcohol are required to create the same effect in suppressing the emotions. Therefore the danger is that a dependency will be created, and one becomes an alcoholic.

Others will escape in sleeping tablets or antidepressants. They look for the same effect, to escape for a while from the severity of the emotion they are going through. To escape into a sphere where emotions do not haunt you. Tablets are also addictive. And quite a few will need a period of rehab. to stop the drink or tablets. I think it is unnecessary to explain that drink and tablets do not give a real solution. The emotions are not dealt with, and are only temporarily suppressed. They will have to be dealt with at a later stage.

Thankfully not everyone will immerse themselves in drink, tablets, or other forms of drugs, but it is the case that they often are a real threat during the grieving process.

So EMPTY

So empty inside
So heavy and so cold
It is as if
I died myself
When, when my beloved
Died. It feels so lifeless
Inside, without warmth
And without feeling

Each day the same:
A winter's day;
The cold lives
In my bones
And although the suns shines
It cannot warm me.

There is no other way
Than through the dark
There is no other way
Than that of patience
I will open again
But when, only
God knows

Each day I pray
Be with me
Carry me in my weakness
Comfort me in my sorrow
Give me the strength
To keep going

In You I put my hope
In You I trust
I wait for You

6.

THE DARK NIGHT, OR PATIENCE, PATIENCE, PATIENCE...

During the grieving process there is a period that might be described as the "dark night." This expression "the dark night" is the title that John of the Cross gave to a hymn and a book. In this book he describes the transformation process of mankind when he looks for God and, in order to find him, begins a struggle with himself and his ego. When a person starts this road deliberately, there is always a period, according to John of the Cross, when you cannot see anything in front of you because of the dark. You will be completely on your own in that period, and there is no one from whom you can expect support. You have no idea how to carry on and what the future will be like. This dark period, during which a person loses everything they can hold onto, is the time when they will learn to trust God alone. If there is no other help, and you cannot find this either from others or from within yourself, than the only help you can hope to receive is the help that comes from God. The dark night is therefore the period in life when all trusted values fall away from us, and we become more sensitive to the reality of God. In this sense, this period is the stage in our life when we lose our learned way of thinking, and find new support in the spiritual reality, a reality of which we may have talked about before, but which only now, in this utter darkness, becomes real. The "dark night" is the essence of the transformation process. In the dark silence, in the depth of the soul, the transformation will take place, and we become different people who are not self-orientated, looking only for our own security, but beings who are focused on God's voice, a voice which we have to hear within our soul and learn to understand.

The grieving process is also a transformation process. It differs from the process as described by John of the Cross, in that it is a transformation process, which we did not choose but that happens anyway. But whatever the situation, through what has happened and everything that comes your way, you will change during the grieving process. The world you lived in has fundamentally changed, and thus you will need to adapt to this new and often much colder world.

When the first severe emotions have come and gone, and when you do not feel the need to talk endlessly with others, when you are turning toward yourself, then the "dark night" will emerge. You can compare this dark night to a tree in the winter. The tree just stands there. It has lost all its leaves, and its life essence has withdrawn to its core. Now it will endure the winter, bare, lifeless, and still. Only in spring, when the sun starts to warm, will new life emerge on the tree. But right now, it is the cold silent wintertime. It appears as if nothing happens during the winter, as if the tree is only waiting for the coming spring. In its deepest core there is a change from the loss that the autumn brought, toward the expectation that the spring will bring. Deep within its core, invisible to the bystander, the tree will live through the process of dying and being reborn. But from the outside you do not see anything; you only see motionless silence. The transformation process takes place completely hidden from anything in the motionless silence of winter.

The dark night in the grieving process is just like the tree. You cannot be bothered with anything and prefer to sit still at home. You feel abandoned, alone, depressed but cannot talk about it because all those feelings are somewhere in the depths of your soul. You don't understand what is happening; there appears to be nothing happening at all. There is only the fundamental feeling of sorrow, which colors everything you do, and see. Each day seems the same, and you feel like that tree in the winter: bereft of all color, fun, and joy. It is a period that seems to go on forever, and you have the feeling that it will never change. You can't do anything other than be patient during this period. Even though it may seem that there are no changes, and that you don't seem to still be in the grieving process, in silence a similar change is working within the deepest parts of your soul, just like the tree in the winter. You die within yourself to be reborn. But you don't see this for yourself. It seems that each day is the same, and that nothing changes for you. That is why you need so much patience, and a lot of stamina. It is a strange silence in which you live, filled with loneliness. What do you have to talk about? You don't even know what happens inside you, or in the depths of your soul. You only know that there is nothing that really interests you. You are active enough, because a lot has to be done. You have to work, you have to cook, you have to talk to others. But it does not interest you, you feel dead inside. You do the things you have to do, because they have to be done, and there is no alternative.

The most difficult part is that you cannot share this with others. If you don't understand it yourself, how could you talk about it with others? The "dark night" appears to be some sort of prison: a boring life, in which, like a prisoner, you do not have much to say; nothing happens but the daily routine. Some people have the feeling that in this lonely stage they edge toward the borderline of what is humanly bearable. The thought that they would rather die will occur to many during this period. They feel empty, and dry, and so intensely sad inside. But it is, and remains, an emptiness and depression, and a powerless feeling that cannot be shared with others. And that is why this stage in the grieving process is really a dark, never-ending night. It is often a period of tears, but of silent tears, of a quiet sadness. The severity of the emotions from the beginning of the grieving process isn't there anymore. There is a feeling of letting go, and not knowing how to go on. The last emotion makes it so difficult for us. The lack of any prospects means that you simply do not see that it ever will, or can be, different. You cannot believe it, as you cannot believe in anything. The only thing to do is to have patience and keep on going day after day.

We can see how the grieving person will turn toward him- or herself during this process. We see that the external supports, in the form of people who come to cheer you up or give you some comfort, fall away. For the others around you it has already become normal that you have lost your loved one. They have accepted this and do not understand – they cannot understand – that you are completely stuck inside yourself, in the dark night that does not seem to pass.

She had lost her husband three years ago. She was only forty-five years old when he died. Both her children had left home and so she was left on her own. For the outside world it appeared that she got used to her new life and also found a new purpose of life. But during the conversation she showed a different side of herself as well when she said, "Each day is a struggle. I have no purpose in life. It could be finished for me tomorrow and I wouldn't shed a tear. There does not appear to be any purpose right now and I have to live on for a while. I suppose that is OK because I know that my children still need me for a while." I could read in her eyes the emptiness and despair, which she could normally hide. "Nobody understands it," she said. "Everyone thinks that I am over it, but I feel so empty and dead inside. Nothing interests me and nothing touches me. I have the feeling that I am going through life like a rag doll."

With those words she described this feeling of the "dark night." The feeling that it will never be different again, a feeling of emptiness, and of an inner world that is dead. In this stage it is very important to understand that this is just a phase of the healing process. It is a phase that seems never-ending, but is in fact a phase that will eventually pass, and will provide a new feeling of life at the end of it all. A new life with a certain expectation, inner peace, and inner warmth will emerge. The insight that the "dark night" is an inevitable phase during the grieving process, and at the same time a passage to a new and more positive life, can provide people with the patience and faith which they need so much in this period.

It is strange that this phase takes the longest, compared with the other stages, but at the same is only a short time during which not much can be said. This is connected with the fact that during this period, the real work is the change within the depths of our soul and so it is hidden.

We don't know how the soul can do this. Perhaps you could say how we are guided in silence, and that the spiritual world works in silence within us so that we can find healing of the heart. That is the secret of the spiritual world. Those who are aware of this will also understand that prayers can provide strength during this time. Regular prayer can help us to find the required courage and patience. Prayer also helps us to regulate the power within our heart with the powers of the spiritual forces, so we receive guidance in the depths of our soul.

More positive emotions will emerge, and stir very slowly in our soul. We notice that we are touched again by someone's warmth. We feel more enthusiasm about things that really interest us. We are often surprised by the fact that different things interest us now. Through the sorrow we have become different people, with other interests and a different view of life. Step by step the transformation, which took place hidden away in our soul, will become visible. A new life will emerge for us and we are led toward this new life through death.

THE MIRACLE OF LIGHT

How is light born?
I don't know how
I don't know, I only know
That you have to work
Very hard for this.

That you need patience
And need to carry on
Even then when there is no prospect
And there appears to be no future

The miracle of light
Is truly a miracle
It is born in silence
Takes place in the depths
Of our soul
It was dark for so long
For a long time, I did
Not know how to continue
I felt despair for so long

But when I lost all hope
Something began to stir
Deep inside me
A feeling so tender and young
I hardly noticed it.

Slowly the spring in me
Grew stronger and I felt hope
I could reconnect myself
With people and the world
Around me

So I was reborn
Step by step

7.
*L*ETTING GO

Growing in strength

We and our loved one, at the moment of death, will go in distinctly different directions. We continue here on earth amidst all its difficulties, but our loved one will start a whole new path of life in the spiritual world. When they start this journey, it is important to allow this path for our loved one, and not keep them back on this earth. Our heart desires the loved one continuously, and therefore we often keep the person alive in our thoughts and desires. At this time we understand more and more that our thoughts and desires have a direct effect on our loved one on the other side. Thoughts and desires are spiritual reality, and our loved one lives in a world where only those spiritual realities are valid. Thoughts and desires are invisible and so we think they do no harm, but within the spiritual world they are a strong and determining force. It is therefore important to allow our loved one this path on their journey beyond death. When our heart calls for the other one continuously, "I wish you were still here," or, "I can't go on without you. Why did you have to go?" those thoughts transform into spiritual forces that work directly in the spiritual world, and make the path of our loved one more difficult. It is as if we place obstacles for their feet on that otherwise so easy path on the other side. That is why our loved ones ask from us a kind of love to "let go," which is not focused on us, but on the other person. They ask if we are truly prepared to allow them this new path in this new world. Of course, this will not happen without sadness. They do not ask us to hide, or feel sorrow. They do ask us if we are prepared, not only to look at our sadness, but also at what is important to them. And that is possible. There can be two feelings in us at the same time, a feeling of loss and grief and, at the same time, a feeling of love in which we allow the other person the new path beyond. The more we realize that the other person becomes him- or herself, becomes the complete human they really are, the more we realize that the other person will now become a being of light in the spiritual world.

We can then feel more and more that we must allow this to happen.

Love requires that we really let go of our loved one and not continuously ask them back. But how do you do that – let go of the other person? Are we capable of doing that? And are you not allowed to look for a sign of life from the spiritual world? Letting go means that you allow the other person their new life, and that you are prepared to continue on this earth without them, that you try to have the courage to make something of your life without them and that you do not continuously desire the past. That is easier said than done: to grow so much that you are capable of doing that doesn't happen overnight. It is a path of trial and error, a path through the dark night. But it is about being prepared from within. You need to be prepared to grow toward that "letting go" so that you can say from the deepest part of your heart: I allow you the path you have to go even though it brings me sorrow.

Letting go: we can learn this, when we try to transform in our being, that part that the other person meant for us. That sounds difficult, I know. But by this I mean that you should try to transform, for instance, the faith and trust the other person had in you into self-confidence. That you learn to look at yourself through the eyes of the other person. That you learn to love yourself, as the other person loved you. That you further develop the characteristics in yourself, which the other person admired in you. The other person will come to life in you; the other will live through you. The more we succeed in absorbing the other person into ourselves, within our being, the easier it becomes to let go of the other person, because they have come to life in us.

That is letting go. Then I don't need the other person for comfort, because I have found comfort with myself. I don't need the other person to confirm myself, because I have found confirmation within myself. I don't need the other person to give me warmth because I am capable of warming myself. When I am capable of doing that then only pure unconditional love will remain. This will make it possible for me to allow the other person that path toward that higher radiant light. When you talk of "letting go" in this way, than it becomes clear that letting go means working hard on yourself, a process through which you become a different, stronger, and more loving person. You bring the other person to life within you by absorbing the gifts you have given the other person in life. We could not give a greater gift to the other person on their path beyond. When they can see, from the other side, what you have accomplished in yourself using all the gifts that they gave to you on earth, then this will stimulate their own journey beyond. They will see this as a reality and their love for us will make them happy to see us grow through the pain of life. And because they live in the spiritual world, only spiritual realities such as our spiritual growth are of prime importance.

That is why it is that you have to become aware of which spiritual gifts the other person gave to you to enrich your life. When you have become aware of this, the next step is to make these gifts a reality for your own being. That is how the spirit of the loved one can awaken in you and enrich you in a new way.

Letting go also means that you learn to develop from that power, and that you learn to live from that power. We are all strong people, much stronger than we give ourselves credit for. God has given each of us a strong primal force. But now, now we are alone, it is important to use this force to really make something of our lives without the other person. Letting go is therefore the opposite of gliding into the abyss of sadness, but through our sorrow our purpose is to grow in self-confidence and strength. Only this strength enables us to hope, and to discover a new purpose in our lives. This strength makes it possible that our loved one on the other side will look upon us with happiness and gratitude, and possible that we will succeed in finding a new way without the other person. The strength enables us to give the other person on the other side the greatest gift of all.

Gratitude

When we learn to let go in this way and let the other person become part of ourselves, when we learn to grow through this in strength and self-confidence, then we discover that a new level of gratitude will emerge in us again. But that feeling of gratitude will be pushed toward the background if sorrow remains at the forefront. The more we learn to let go, and the more we succeed in finding our own way, the more this feeling of gratitude, purified and matured through the sorrow, will come to the forefront.

First of all there is gratitude for all that our loved one has given us, the way they enriched our lives. We become aware that without what was given by the other person we could not become the human beings we are now. But also we have gratitude that we did not succumb to the sorrow and that it did not destroy us, but that, as through a miracle in the loneliness and silence of the dark night, we received help and guidance to succeed in finding the way forward, albeit with difficulties. And finally, gratitude for all we discovered and learned in this dark time; when everything has improved a whole new world has opened for us, and we have received spiritual insights which enriched our lives. We discovered our own answer to the question of death: what is death, and what will happen to our loved one on the other side? To this question we found, and still find, our own answer, even though we can hardly find the words to express what we know in our soul. And even though the quest for answers is difficult – sometimes we know, and sometimes it appears that we have lost it again – we do discover that the answers become a reality in our hearts.

Besides this, we have become different people through dealing with loss and sorrow. The more we can see how we have changed, the greater the feeling of gratitude that awakens in us. Gratitude is also growing in us when we discover how we were guided in the darkest period of our lives. Gratitude knows how to value all the gifts we received. Just past the middle of the tunnel, all those feelings start to waken again. In the beginning, very slowly and tenderly. But the further on we go, the more this feeling of gratitude awakens in us as a real spiritual strength. It is this strength, this growing gratitude, which will lead us through the last phases of the tunnel.

You must realize that gratitude cannot be forced. It grows. But it always grows where we are working on the process of letting go in a serious way. Incidentally, this gratitude is never of the joyous kind that we may have known in the past together with our loved one. This time the gratitude has more the color of silent knowing. It is more like the richness of autumn rather than the exuberance of spring.

Releasing love

I cannot emphasize enough the importance of letting go. This letting go process starts immediately the moment our loved one dies. Our loved one stands at the beginning of a new path, which may be intimidating – in particular when death came unexpectedly, and our loved one was confronted with this new life and new path in an unexpected way. But even our loved one was able to prepare themselves for this change if, for example, a short or long illness preceded the death. Despite this the new situation can still be intimidating. This new path must now begin for real, and they must learn to continue without the help and companionship of their earthly loved ones. I have to say that on the threshold, others are there to greet our loved ones and guide their ways. These could be loved ones who have already died. But the closeness of those loved ones, the angels, and Christ does not take the fact away that our loved one has to let go of us as well, just as we have to let go of them. They must let go of the earthly world, and thus of all who were dear to them, in this world. At least for a while, because we see each other at a later stage. Just as our new life without our loved one is not easy, so it is not easy for our loved one on the other side. But the light of that greater spiritual world beckons, and is enticing, and those who greeted the loved one first when they arrived in this world encourage them to make the first steps on this new path.

But if the people who are left behind begin to call them back, then it becomes more difficult. If they say or think that they cannot go on without the other person, then the loved one feels recalled and often tries to go back in vain.

> I once attended a funeral. The coffin with the body of the deceased stood at the front of the church, because the burial was to take place after the church service. During the funeral service various people said in so many ways that the people who were left behind would miss the deceased loved one, and that they did not know how to continue without her. I could suddenly see the deceased come floating toward the coffin, obviously with the intention of entering the dead body. She was called through the voices of her loved ones who had said that they could not continue without her, and that is why she wanted to return. But then I suddenly saw two angels before the coffin with raised swords. Those swords crossed each other and prevented the deceased woman

from gaining access to the body. Then just as suddenly as it appeared the image was gone again. It made clear to me how everything we say or think has an influence on the deceased. Later, during the condolences, I overheard people saying how touching the whole service had been. At that moment I felt sorry that I could not share what I had seen with others.

Letting go starts, therefore, immediately after the death of the loved one. If we really love the other person, then a releasing love is requested: a love that allows the other person, who has embarked on this new path, to travel this path in a real sense. We may express this releasing love again and again, not only during the funeral, but also in the way we talk about our loved one to others, at a later stage. We may express in those conversations that we allow our loved one this new path even though we may still feel the pain of the loss. We may express that we do not wish that the other person was back, no matter how painful this may be.

The darkness begins to fade

When we have learned how to let go and the other person has become (for a bit at least) part of us, and when gratitude begins to emerge besides our feelings of sorrow, then light is also sometimes visible in the tunnel that was hitherto dark. There is light at the end of the tunnel at last. It means that we will also feel less isolated, that we don't feel an outsider and a stranger in a world that has become completely incomprehensible. There still aren't many people, of course, whom you can talk to about the thing that stirs inside your soul. There aren't many people around who understand anything of letting go, not many people who understand how something like gratitude can grow in the darkness. There aren't many people with whom you can share how you experience your connection with the deceased person, and how you felt the presence of your loved one. But thankfully, they do exist, and just sometimes when you feel you want to share something that stirs inside you, you feel and learn how to connect with people again, where before you only felt like an outsider. The strange thing is, as many have said who have experienced this, that when you start to tell someone about what is inside you, the other person often opens their heart and starts to tell you things that they have never said to anyone before. In this way you receive a new gift, you discover that you are able to touch the other person in their hearts and move them. You discover that the other person trusts you so much that they disclose their life secret. Many reveal that during this phase of the grieving process they discovered that they were able to listen far better to the life secrets that others disclosed. It is as if they listened with a different intention, deeper and with more real attention and more understanding. Those who have experienced the darkness in their own life and have been able to keep going are not afraid any more of the darkness in the life of others, but are capable of sharing this and this loving sharing process will shine light in the darkness.

Of course, the feeling of being an outsider or a stranger has not disappeared straight away, and in a certain way it will always be that way. Because if you have gone through the darkness, you will have discovered what really matters in life and what is unimportant. And everywhere you will meet people who are bothered about unimportant things and when this happens you will feel an outsider. But you can say that someone who has discovered how to share with a select few what stirs inside has made a start with a new and different way in which they learn to connect with people.

Many who are marked through the loss of a loved one, with all the sorrow connected with this, will discover that you can be a victor in that darkness with real consolation, and real attention.

YOU LIVE WITHIN ME

I feel, you live within me
You will never die
You live forever
In my heart

You have made me rich, I see
Looking back, I only now see
How rich. And still
You work in me,
Make me strong and loving

The greater the distance
Between you and me
The more I see
What you gave me
With your love
And what you still give.

You live within me
And at the same time

You live in the space
Of the spiritual world
Guarded and protected
Through the light of this
From there you work
In and through me
Because love is forever
And is a force
Which never dies

8.

*T*O OPEN AGAIN FOR LIFE

Light at the end of the tunnel

It is difficult to tell when the end of the tunnel is in sight. It is even harder to tell the end of the grieving process. It comes gradually, and is almost unnoticeable. It is certainly not the case that you can say: today I will take the last step in this tunnel, and tomorrow the grieving process is finally over. In some ways the sorrow will never pass. There always will be days, and shorter or longer periods, when the memories of our loved one will come back to us and when we feel that the sorrow and loss has a new grip on us. You only need to see, quite by accident, an old photograph, and straight away the whole day will be tainted by the memories recalled by it.

The end of the tunnel comes in sight when we start to feel, when we open ourselves again for the abundance of spring, or for the colorful displays of the autumn, when we feel touched by all this abundance and beauty, and experience this not from the outside, but in our inner soul. The end is in sight when we start to smile, and when faces of people begin to touch us; when we are touched by feelings of hope, expectation, purity, and love, which we may read in those faces. The fact that we can be touched is a process that does not happen from one day to another. We just discover one day that it is something that has simply happened and entered our life. We discover that we can allow ourselves to be vulnerable again, and that is truly a miracle when you become aware of it after such a long time. However, there is another task awaiting us. There are people who become frightened when they laugh for the first time. They feel it as a betrayal of the deceased loved one, as if they are being unfaithful when they take part in life again. There are also people who find it difficult to let go of their sorrow, not only because they feel that it is a betrayal, but also because a kind of emptiness will come over them. You first have to let go of the old before the new can be born. And that is why you have to go through the emptiness before life can be felt again within you. It requires willpower to allow yourself emotions and vulnerability. It requires an inner decision to trust yourself to this new life. But when you make this decision, and when you realize that to take part in life in a new way is not a betrayal of the other person, it actually does good to your loved one. Then you will experience how life will become brighter, bit by bit, and how sorrow does not have a grip on you all the time. Then you will feel that there is definitely light at the end of the tunnel.

This means that you also start to reconnect with people in a different way, that you don't feel an outsider any longer, like someone with a different inner world from the rest of mankind. You feel that you belong again in a different way because through the grieving process you have become a different person. You have matured, often becoming milder, and with more understanding, and you have learned to become interested in different things. This often means that you will meet different people from those you knew before, and that there will be changes in your circle of friends. You also discover, for example with the loss of a child, that you become interested again in other children, your attention is no longer purely focused on the one child you had lost. You will get space to think again about a new life partner, if you have lost your partner. You get space again for new friendships, and begin to enjoy them again. That is how you experience becoming connected again with life, as you change from an outsider to someone who takes part in life in their own way.

The wealth of poverty

How long does the grieving process take? In a book, published in the USA, written by two authors, a man and a woman who had both lost their partners, the conclusion was that it took about 4 months to go through the grieving process. In Europe, it was concluded, more then a year. It is possible that dealing with grief goes faster in the US than in Europe: the cultural background is different. But in Europe it will take quite a bit longer than one expects: five years rather than one year. You would like it to go faster. You would like it to be finished within one year. But the end of the grieving process is not something you control with your will. It has to do with the processing speed of your soul, and the soul does not take into account what your personal wishes or desires are. Our soul is as breakable as thin porcelain. That is why our soul requires lots and lots of time to deal with the depth of our loss and to transform us, bit by bit, into another human being, which is something that always happens when we go through our pain and sorrow. Our soul moves forward, millimeter by millimeter, and it cannot go faster, otherwise it would break. That is why it is understandable that the grieving process takes five years rather than one. It is important to really have the patience for this process. It is essential because we may not be able to realize the silent wealth, which we gain during this process. We must allow our soul the time to become aware of the silent wealth and put this in our heart.

But what is this silent wealth, which is brought to us during this journey through the dark night, and the journey through the tunnel? It takes many different forms. First it can be found in the manner in which we have made the loved one a part of ourselves: how we have assimilated the insights and ways of life from our loved one into our being. Through this our inner strength and self-confidence grows, and we need these to simply survive the grieving process. The next bit of wealth can be experienced in the way we have learned a growing understanding for others who are struck by sorrow and despair: We have become more sensitive, milder, wiser, and less intolerant than we used to be. And finally, our silent wealth can be found in the way we have learned to look upon death: our growing insights, for instance, that there is always a connection between us and the loved one. The insight, that death is not the end, but only a new beginning in another dimension, in another world. The insight that we will meet each other again, and that, even though we live in different worlds, we can take care of each other.

Once again I emphasize here that everyone who has gone through the grieving process will say that the gain of those silent riches is nice and very special, but that they would have preferred to gain them in a different way, without having to miss the loved one. That is why you describe this inner wealth as the wealth of our poverty.

The process of living through the grieving process belongs, in a certain way, to the "higher education" part of life: here all your spiritual resources are required, here you will deal with all the essences of life, here you will learn all the things which really matter, but here also all our attention is required to succeed in the task which the academy of life has put upon us. And the certificate from this academy of life is more precious then any other diploma. Even though many would argue that they would rather miss this diploma than have to lose their dearest in order to gain it. You may speak about gains, and thus light, when you have taken the darkness and the pain of the grieving process very seriously indeed.

The schedule of Kubler-Ross

Elisabeth Kubler-Ross – whom I mentioned earlier – has described in her famous book *Teachings for the Living* the various stages, which someone who is about to die will go through. The four main stages she identifies are: the stage of denial, the stage of anger, the stage of depression, and the stage of surrender. (Between the first two and the last two stages, she mentions a kind of phase in between, which she calls the bargaining phase.) In some way those four phases can also be applied to the grieving process. That is rather understandable since preparation for death is also to live through the grieving process. You grieve about the life here on earth, and which you have to let go, and about the people you love and have to leave behind. If you work through the chapters of this book as you are now doing, you will have noticed that the same base pattern of Kubler-Ross is also the base of this book. You might not have noticed this, because many people who go through the grieving process say that they haven't noticed these different phases, which Kubler-Ross describes, at all. Their own experience is not so much a clear and recognizable process, where you grow from one phase into another, but rather that of chaos, which is hard to understand or to comprehend. Life itself is not a schedule, and the living reality is always more chaotic than a schedule. Moreover, the grieving process is more a question of survival, the difficulty of starting each day and bearing the chill and intense loneliness, rather than being able to distinguish a clear cool pattern in all those emotions.

But the schedule of Kubler-Ross can provide some assistance. Looking back, everyone who is confronted with the sudden death of a loved one, can look at how long it took before it really sank into the depths of their heart that their loved one had died and would never come back. Looking back, many will recognize the stage of denial, just as many will recognize the stage of anger, the depression, the acceptance and the surrender, which is described by Kubler-Ross. But this recognition and arranging, we find much later when we look back and not when we are in the middle of it. The most important contribution of the schedule of Kubler-Ross for me is the hope and the prospect that there can be a time when you will get peace in your life again. There can be a time when you can even enjoy your life. There can be a time when you will experience warmth and love, and you can admit that to your heart. The schedule provides courage and strength to keep going, even when the darkness of the tunnel seems without an end and the loneliness is unbearable.

The grieving process; a very personal path

It is often said that men and women deal with the grieving process differently. It is said that women are focused on the relationship, and live through the connection with their loved ones. That is why they lose a grip on things with the death of a loved one, as if the ground falls away beneath their feet. The relationship with the deceased is an essential part of life for them. For men this is often different. They say that they exist to put something of themselves into the world. A woman is open toward the outside world, while a man is more focused and tries to take something from the inside to the outside. The man will go through the grieving process in a different way. He does not talk much about his personal feelings and experiences. He prefers to do something rather than to talk. And so you often see that men throw themselves into various little jobs in order to try to keep their inner balance. However, we have to be careful about generalizations; there are women who have a more male attitude and men who have a more female attitude. Furthermore, there is a cultural and social shift going on, through which the differences between men and women appear to be diminishing. Nevertheless we can still recognize the differences in the process in daily life. Women often need to talk about their loved one; men will say that they are always talking about the same thing over and over again and do not appear to move forward. They can move forward, they say, because their ego can deal with it in a better way. Men prefer to go on as quickly as they can with the order of the day, in order to find some grip in their lives, and women say that men try to escape their feelings and emotions. But this is not true either, because men find solace in structure, and in work, bearing their sorrow and their loss in silence. Joke Forcevill, who wrote various books about the grieving process after the death of her husband, wrote, "I have often seen how men could heal from their grief with the love of a new woman." But, she writes, women want to deal with their sorrow first before they can go into a new relationship. These differences alone already indicate how differently the grieving process may go. What is good for one is not good for another. In the grieving process, in particular, everyone has to listen to their inner voice, to find guidance on that difficult path through the dark.

I DON'T KNOW

I don't know
How I came through
I don't know

Don't ask me
What I thought
And felt
I don't know

I only know
That I didn't
Know the way
That each day
Was difficult
That each day
Was a day too many
How it became bright?
I don't know
All I know is
That I was retained
Helped and guided

By whom?
I don't know
But each morning
I say: Thanks

9.

DREAMS DURING THE GRIEVING PROCESS

During the grieving process, and also afterwards, many people will have dreams during which their loved one will appear. These dreams will often make a deep and lasting impression. These dreams have two functions, or rather two meanings, and it is important to distinguish both. First, they are processing dreams: dreams that will help us to deal with our sorrow and to accept that our loved one has really died. It can take a long time before the death of the loved one is accepted in the innermost depths of our soul. We know that our beloved has died, but our soul has not accepted it. Therefore, during the first period immediately after the death of the loved one, we receive dreams in which they will appear just like old times, coming home from work or cooking the dinner. Or we receive dream images of the child who is playing just as if nothing has happened, and everything we experienced was like a bad dream. It will take a while before we have dream images about the death of our loved one and the funeral or cremation. When these images appear, then we know that our soul can finally accept the fact that the death is irreversible and that our loved one will never come back, at least not in this life.

That is how processing dreams can help us to understand how far we have come in the grieving process, and to what degree our soul has accepted it all. In this sense, our dreams are an indicator and reflection of our progress through the dark tunnel of sorrow. But there are also other types of dreams. Dreams in which we are allowed to experience a message from our loved one, from the other side. A woman whose daughter died five weeks after her birth told me that two years later she had the following dream.

> In my dream I saw my little daughter in a beautiful wooden coffin, with beautiful white flowers around her head. She was dead, but she looked beautiful. I thought: there you are, she is really dead. But then suddenly she sat up and looked at me, beaming and smiling. Then she said: "I am not dead at all, I am alive."

This dream makes clear that the mother had accepted in herself the death of her daughter to the depths of her souls. She was finally aware: she is dead and will never come back. The beginning of this dream reflects the acceptance of death. But then suddenly her daughter appears to live and tells her mother, beaming, that she is not dead, but alive. Exactly at that moment, when the mother has accepted the inevitable truth, something else has been revealed to her, that death is not the end but that our loved ones live on, on the other side in another dimension, in a different way. The mother told me that this dream had made a deep impression on her and that she would never forget it.

Philosophical traditions tell us that dreams are much more than just dreams. During our sleep we leave our body and enter the spiritual world. We will remember what we experienced and what we have done the next day, vaguely, as a dream. We can also recognize the fact that we leave our body and come back the next morning by the shock that we sometimes feel when we wake up. That shock is caused because our spiritual bodies do not always glide with ease back into our material bodies but "land" sometimes with a bit of bump.

Some people also experience the fact that moments before they really wake up, they cannot move their hands, feet, anything at all. They cannot turn round in the bed. That is because their spiritual bodies are not fully connected yet to the material body. A bit of patience is required and, after a while, they can move again and open their eyes.

If we can realize that this takes place, then it becomes understandable that some dreams about a deceased person are in fact the reflection of a real meeting in the spiritual world with the deceased loved one. During our out-of-the-body experience we entered the spiritual world where our loved one met us. In the above dream, the mother has really met her daughter, and her daughter has given her a message herself that death is not the end, but the beginning of a new life. And if the daughter looks at her mother with a radiant smile, then it means that life on the other side is also a radiant life. Therefore it is understandable that this dream made such an impression on the mother and that she would never forget it. How could you ever forget the reunion with a loved one? Another woman, whose husband had died seven months previously, dreamt the following.

In my dream I climbed the stairs. Then I suddenly saw my husband at the top of the stairs. He looked much younger, and had blond hair instead of brown. He did not see me, but I saw him. I just looked at him and thought: yes, it is really him.

The woman who dreamt this, climbed stairs. The stairs symbolize the out-of-body experience and the ascension to a higher dimension than the reality on earth. And there she sees her husband. Her husband looks much younger in her dream. That is something that happens a lot in dreams about deceased loved ones. When we see something of their new life, we see them in the strength of their youth, between thirty and thirty-five years old. Beyond death there is no age, no decay, no death. There we become the strong people we once were, not in a physical but in a spiritual sense. That is why we see our elder deceased loved ones as younger people in our dreams.

The woman also notices that her husband's hair is not brown, but blond. That blond hair symbolizes the power of light on the other side of death. It also symbolizes our life force. Think about the Bible story of Samson, whose special powers disappeared when his hair was shaved off. The blond hair of the man in the above dream, symbolizes the fact that he is alive in the brightness of the spiritual world and that he is no longer alive in the worldly sense.

Not all dreams about the deceased are true meetings. Sometimes we do not ascend in our dreams toward the higher spheres, but remain in the lower spheres where we receive images that help us to deal with what has happened in our lives. An example of such a processing dream is the next one from a woman, who for years cared for her mother who had a long-term illness. A year after her mother's death she had this dream.

In my dream, I still have to care for my mother. Sometimes I noticed how her face was distorted by pain. I also saw how sad she was, and how thin and degenerated through her illness. I cannot shake this image off.

This dream image is a clear reflection of what the daughter experienced with her mother during her illness. It does not say anything about her new life on the other side of death, but does say everything about life before death, and especially about the way her daughter had experienced it.

The daughter is only now able to start to deal with what she experienced during the years she looked after her mother. She only now begins to feel the sorrow and pain of the decay of her mother. It is possible that when her mother was still alive there was no room for those feelings. She had to be strong, because she had to care, and there was no time to give way to her sorrow. But now, a year after her mother's death, there is at last the space and time to feel, and to deal with what she could not feel at the time. Therefore this is a typical processing dream. It is important to recognize the difference between a typical processing dream and a real meeting. If the daughter thought that the above dream was a real meeting, then she could think that her mother was still ill and sad on the other side.

A woman dreamt the following, three months after the death of her husband.

I came into a hall, which appeared to be a party hall, filled with joyous and happy people. In the midst of all those

people I saw my husband. He wore beautiful clothes.
They were new and had a green color, the kind of green
that was his favorite. He had a glass of water in his hand.
I found that very strange since during his life on earth he
detested water. He always said: water is for frogs.

The woman told me that this dream was very reassuring for her,
and that this was a message that her husband was happy in his new
life, which had now begun for him. The details of the dream are
speaking volumes: he wears new clothes, and those clothes are his
favorite color. The clothes symbolize his new appearance and his
new view on life, which he has learned in the spiritual world. Water
is the symbol of that new life, everlasting life. In the Bible water is
mentioned as the water of life and we speak about it that way. The
water is the symbol of that new spiritual life. We can say that this
is a meeting dream, even though the husband did not see her in the
dream and they did not speak to each other. But the fact that she
could see him and saw with her own eyes that he was alright, was
enough.

A woman dreamt the following after the death of her husband
four years earlier.

I came into a strange house in which my husband was
also present. He had a boy on his arm, but the strangest
thing was that this boy appeared to be born from him.
He did not say that, but I instinctively knew that to be
the case. He offered the child to me but I panicked at
what I saw. This was not possible? A child could not be
born from a man?

This dream is also a real meeting. The man has a child, born from himself. A child in our dream always symbolizes new possibilities and new life forces born within us. It is therefore always a positive symbol for renewing forces. The fact that the man has a child in the spiritual world, means that he has gone through transformation and a renewing process. He has become a new and different person. Then the man gives the child to the woman: that means that he wants to give her something of his new life force. That is something we often see, both in dreams and in messages from the deceased. Those who have gone on to the spiritual world often feel the need to help those who are left behind, and to give something of what they received from the other side. They are connected with us, and want to help us through the different way that has become possible for them. They want to help us through inspiration so that we can realize our life potential. Not for nothing did someone say to his wife before he died: "Remember I can do more for you there than over here," and that is true by all accounts. But because those gifts, from our loved one, are always invisible and given in silence without conscious knowledge, we often don't see them. That is why, unfortunately, we do not recognize what our loved ones do for us from the spiritual world.

In the above dream, the woman panicked because the man gives her the child. She cannot comprehend that her husband has something to give from the spiritual world. Most of us cannot comprehend this, because this knowledge has become lost in our times. How is it possible that a deceased loved one can do something for us? But the dream says clearly that it is possible and that the husband really does this: he gives his wife the child, new spiritual strength.

From these few dreams it becomes clear how dreams can help us in the grieving process. They help us by processing and telling us how far we have traveled on that difficult path through the dark tunnel. Beside this, our dreams can provide us with comfort and new insights, when we have a meeting with our loved ones in our dreams. We should not forget that our loved ones live now with a greater knowledge. The restrictions of earthly life have fallen away and with this also the shortsightedness. They can see the life task of their loved ones who remain on earth, and love will bring them toward their loved ones with inspiration and guidance. This assistance is hidden, but that does not mean it is less true. Love is everlasting, and death can bring no end to that. The love only changes in color and appearance, but it remains constant.

I KNOW

I know: you are alive
There in the land of light
You are not dead
You are alive
I know it
With my heart

I know: the love
Which binds us never dies
Love cannot die
Because she is everlasting
That is why we
Remain connected

In love
You over there, me here

I know: you care
For me
From that land
Where you now live
You can see
What is hidden,
You can see the lesson of life
Which I have yet to learn
The task
Which I have to fulfill
And with all your strength
You inspire me
And help me

I know:
You are not dead
You are alive
I send you
All the love
From my heart
So that you can feel
That our love is everlasting

10.

A REMAINING CONNECTION

In closing this book I would like to say something about the connection that remains between those who remain on earth and their deceased loved ones. From American research, as I mentioned earlier, it was concluded that more than 50 per cent of people who had lost a loved one, had received a sign of love after the death occurred. More than 50 per cent! Strangely enough, this fact does not draw a lot of attention, probably because it is not taken seriously. Outsiders cannot imagine such experiences, and see it as fantasy or wishful thinking.

But for those who have received such a sign of life from the other side of death, it is clear: our connection with our loved ones does not end with death, but is continued on a different, higher, spiritual level. Philosophical traditions are very clear about this remaining connection: love is everlasting and cannot die. Our loved ones enter a new spiritual world to continue their journey, but from that world, they remain connected with all whom they loved on earth. Just as we carry our loved ones in our heart on earth so will our loved ones carry us in their heart.

They can also see, from their greater knowledge that is their part, what our life task is and why we came on this earth. And because they can see that now, they can also send us the help we need to fulfill our task in the correct way. We may not be able to touch our loved ones and hug them and there may be no real presence but yet, they can inspire us in a new spiritual way and guide us. They wrap us in their love and knowledge. It is not for nothing that it is said that our loved ones can do more for us from the spiritual world than when they were with us in material body.

If you can accept this knowledge, then you can feel something of the greatness of this new connection with our deceased loved one. We can also assist our loved ones on the other side. We can send them everlasting love and inspiration, to help them find their path toward the light, where their real home is.

Love does not die, love will stay alive, even though one may live here on earth and the other in the spiritual world, and that is why we remain connected, wherever we are. Our connections and our love relationship will remain and go on, only the sphere and interpretation of this connection changes. That is the surprising light thrown on the question by philosophical traditions; that people on earth do remain connected with their deceased loved ones.

But what can we do here for our loved ones who are dead? In order to understand that, we have to realize that our loved ones live in a spiritual world, and that the connection only takes place on a spiritual level. Those spiritual impulses are decisive for our loved ones in their new world. But what are those spiritual forces and impulses that they can receive, even though they live in a world behind a shroud? This, for example: our loved ones hear all we say and know all we think. Because our spoken or thought words are spiritual forces, which can be heard not only on earth but also in the spiritual world, our loved ones remain accessible. Many people find this difficult to understand, because we are not used to it in our western culture. But philosophy tells us that it is so. And many have experienced, also in our present time, that words which they spoke were unexpectedly answered immediately by their loved ones on the other side of death. That reply came sometimes as an audible voice from outside, but often as a clearly recognizable inner voice. But to those who experienced it, it was an inner certainty: this is their loved one.

Philosophy tells us that there are three main spiritual impulses with which we can help our loved ones on the other side with inspiration. Those three are, of course, the impulse of our *everlasting love*, the impulse of our *thanks* for what we have received during the life of our loved one, and the impulse of *courage*, which we need in order to continue here on earth without the close proximity of our deceased loved one. Obviously, these spiritual gifts are not the same for everyone.

How can you feel love when all is dead inside, because you feel so sad and alone? How can you be thankful if you have suffered such a big loss? And where do you find the courage to go on, on this earth? The spiritual gifts that we can give to our loved one after their death are not obvious and easy. You have to work hard to be thankful, among all the sorrow and loss, that you met this person during your life. And you have to work hard to find the courage to continue without the other person and to make something of your life. Only those who do not become bitter and resentful, but who have the courage to go through the tears of loss and sorrow, will be able to find such thanks and courage. Only those people will be able to provide their loved ones on the other side with some spiritual inspiring gifts on their journey. Thus we see that we can really give the other person something on their journey and remain close and connected, if we do not avoid our pain and loss, but if we are prepared to go through this. Only those who are prepared to go through this will gain this gratitude and courage through the loss and sadness.

It is very difficult to realize that spiritual gifts really reach the other person on the other side of death, and to believe that those gifts are really important for our loved ones. But don't forget, our loved ones will think about us just as we think about them. And that is why it will do them good, if they can experience our heartfelt inspiration for them on their new life journey. It is a true stimulant and real joy for them, if they receive our gratitude, our courage, and our love. It will make their journey so much easier, more joyful and brighter.

Philosophical traditions tell us that we can give our loved ones these gifts all the time. During a nice walk through the forest, you can think about your loved one and recall a memory that will make you warm inside. And from this warmth you can send continuing love and gratitude from your heart toward your loved one. It will reach the other person directly. You can also do this during a prayer, a meditation, or just before you go to sleep. It only matters that you are very aware, with all your inner attention, and are silent, so that you really can send love to the other side. And, as I said, it will work directly. *Each spiritual act from our heart works directly in the spiritual world and sets spiritual forces in motion.*

But how does our loved one stay in connection with us from that other unseen world? How do they live with us? And what can they actually do for us? With all these questions it is important to know how loved ones can see us from the spiritual world. Because they certainly can see us, but very differently from when they were in their body on earth. Then they looked at our faces, they looked at the expression on our faces and in our eyes. They saw what we did and heard what we said. That's the way they got to know us, and that is how they lived with us. But now in the spiritual world they have no eye for the physical body. They see the body as a vague mist. But what was hidden from them during their life on earth, our inside, and what happened in our heart, that is what they see now. The inside of us is our spiritual reality, and from the spiritual world our loved ones have a sharper eye for the spiritual truth. They can see right through the mist of our body, and see the movements within our heart, and see everything that is going on. And what they see will touch them. They see, for instance, the wisdom and insight, which we gain through our sorrow. And this will be a revelation to them, which will give them new insight. They learn to be with us. Our insights become their insights and are gifts to them.

What I write here is something special: namely that our loved ones can learn and grow through a permanent connection with our heart and through what they can take from our heart to them. It is therefore striking, since they now live in a world of wisdom that they can take in themselves in a very direct way. So why do they need our wisdom in order to grow? Because our wisdom and insight is unique. They are gained with pain, sorrow, and the struggle with our own ego. That is why earthly wisdom is a unique wisdom, which you can only learn on earth. Wisdom in the spiritual world is a direct wisdom, which flows into our hearts, but earthly wisdom is a conscious wisdom because it is gained through all those dark forces that live on earth. That is why our loved ones on the other side are still growing in conscious wisdom, which they may take from us through their own heart.

It is also the case that our loved ones, behind the veil now, can see what our life task is. And from the greater knowledge they speak in silence to our heart, encouraging us and trying to inspire us so that we can reach those goals in those life tasks for which we have come. They learn from our wisdom, but they give us in turn their covering of permanent love and inspiration.

As a clairvoyant I have often experienced that deceased individuals, whom I did not know, came to me to ask if I could give a message to someone here on earth. As soon as they stood in the room I knew immediately: oh, that is the father of so-and-so or that is the daughter of that person. In the spiritual dimension you do not need to introduce yourself, because it is a telepathic knowledge. I discovered in those meetings that it is very important for the deceased loved ones to reach the ones who are left behind in their hearts and to connect with them. I also discovered that they are really looking for their loved ones to open themselves on earth in their hearts and to allow the connection for their love and invisible presence. Because only if the one who is left behind opens their heart, can their loved ones reach them, and only then can they experience a permanent connection. It therefore depends on us whether our loved ones on the other side of death are allowed to feel connected with us in a permanent way. It is very sad for the deceased loved one (I cannot find a better way to express this), if we pretend that dead is dead, if we do not realize that the connection in love goes on in a different, new, and spiritual way. Because then we break off this connection, and that hurts our loved ones on the other side. That is why some of them ask me to bring messages to their loved ones, so that the connection can be restored. And then, when we have opened ourselves up to our loved ones, than they can wrap us in the strength of their higher self or with the power of the hidden Christ in them. Because that higher self, or that hidden Christ, is set free and comes into the light of their journey through the spiritual world. With those great divine powers, they want to help us. But, as I have said, it is only possible if we have opened the channel for those silent powers ourselves, and we must be ready to receive those gifts.

The most important gift that we can give to our loved ones, and thus to ourselves, is to be ready to receive this permanent connection and so to be touched by the tender and loving forces in which they want to wrap us.